THE STATLER BROTHERS
Random Memories

Harold Reid and Don Reid

Published in Nashville, Tennessee, by Yell Publishing Company.

Front cover photograph by Charles Clemmer.
Design by Garrett Rittenberry, guerrilla design.
Copy editing by Pamela Lee Grau

ISBN 978-0-9800883-0-4

Printed in the United States of America

To Debbie

"Many women do
noble things,
but you surpass them all."
Proverbs 31:29

Don

For Brenda

This to
The love of my wife
Which is
The love of my life

With love,
Harold

And to
Mom and Dad
There are no words
— Buck and Pete

INTRODUCTION

We don't like long and boring introductions, so this won't be one. But before you begin reading the following pages, we want you to know that this book was never meant to be an official history of the Statler Brothers and each of its members. It was never meant to be an in-depth look at our personal lives and our families. It is what the title says it is—Random Memories of ours—of the things we did, the places we went, and the people we met along the way. We hope you enjoy what we had to say and the way we said it. We tried to touch on what we thought was important, interesting and entertaining. We went to great effort to make sure every word was true, never depending on our memories when we had records and never letting our hearts get in the way of a good story.

We hope you enjoy reading it as much as we did living it.

— Harold Reid and Don Reid

statlerbrothers.com

Chapter One

Times may come and times may go
Through stages, phases and fads
But we'll be here as souvenirs
Of all the times we had

— Don Reid

"The Times We Had"

— Don —

The final weekend was Huntsville, Alabama; Asheville, North Carolina; and Salem, Virginia—just 90 miles from home. It was planned that way. We always tried to end a tour as close to home as possible so we made a special effort to end our career as close to home as possible. Yes, in answer to many questions at the time, it could have been in Staunton, Virginia, our hometown, but it would have had to have been outside as there's no venue big enough and October in the Shenandoah Valley can be an unreliable friend. We even found that July in the Valley can be unreliable, but that's another chapter and one we will get to soon enough.

So it was Huntsville on Thursday, October 24, 2002, and it was the beginning of the ending that we had been working toward for the past year. Maybe for the past 38 and a half years, although I dare say that first night that we count as the beginning of our professional career—March 8, 1964, in Canton, Ohio, with the Johnny Cash show—did we have in our heads how it would all end. We were too busy getting started and too ambitious to think it would ever end or that we would ever want it to. But here we were, back-

1

stage in Huntsville, on the bus and getting dressed to go on as we had thousands of times before. The only thing different about it tonight was that we knew it wouldn't be a thousand times more. Ever since we had announced publicly back the first of January that this would be our last year of touring, we had looked at everything we did, every town we played, every hotel lobby, and every fan on the front row and realized that this would be the last time we would be seeing these places and people. How many times through the years had we stayed at the Huntsville Hilton and how many times had I walked and run that little park across the street? I knew the sidewalk by heart. The dressing rooms were imbedded in our minds just like the ones in Evansville or Peoria or Tucson or any other mid to major city in the U.S., Canada and Europe. They had become our home on the road. We had friends in each of these towns even though we may not know their names. They were good and loyal people who had supported us for years; bought the records; watched the TV show; come to the concerts. And they were here tonight in full force. And then there were friends backstage whose names we *did* know. They'd come from not-far-away Nashville to give their goodbyes and hugs and good wishes. And we gave them ours. And I think the heaviest thought we carried with us as we pulled out of there late on that Thursday night with the bus lights low in the lounge and the shades pulled for privacy, was that we were going to have to do this two more times and probably, just probably, it was going to get harder each night.

We checked into Asheville at 6 a.m. the next morning. This was our pattern. We found years ago that it was easier to travel at night. Traffic was less and it was less hassle for us to go into truck stops or 24-hour grocery stores in the middle of the night than in the middle of the day. So our drivers (we had two drivers and two who relieved on our two tour buses) would sleep in the daytime and travel all night. And so did we. The music and touring business is akin to the burglary and robbery business. It's mostly done at dark and the daytime is for the 'normal' folks. We never felt normal on the road. At home we worked hard to achieve a sense of normalcy, but once on tour, we had to become a different animal to survive.

Friday night there were more friends backstage who had come to say goodbye. My wife, Debbie, was with me on the bus. Brenda, Wilma, and Nina—Harold's, Phil's, and Jimmy's wives respectively—would join us tomorrow at the hotel in Salem. We would do the same show we did last night and the same we'd do the 'last night.' The first of the month we had added "Amazing Grace" as the final song and Asheville was actually the tenth time we had closed with it and we should have become used to it, but each night it was touching a few more nerves and emotions in us than the night before.

The ride from Asheville to Salem would be the last four hours we would ever spend together on the bus. It had become a routine in winding down after a concert; we would eat a late supper in the lounge and watch the news as we rode and then usually put in a movie till we started falling out one by one and heading to the back to our individual quarters and going to bed. And like countless nights before, in the middle of a peaceful sleep, Marshall Grant, our agent and road manager, would stop in the aisle at our bunks and say, "We're here," and we'd get up in the wee hours (this particular morning 2:30 a.m.) and go in the back door of a hotel that he had already pre-checked us into. Some mornings you could fall back asleep immediately once you hit the bed but way too often that walk to the room would get you awake to where you'd be staring at a TV with nothing but infomercials to entertain you till well past dawn. As I think I've already said, there's nothing normal about life on the road.

That last day at the hotel was very much like all the other hotel days had been over the past four decades—quiet and conducive to reading. A little running in the late morning and room service in the early afternoon so that you never went on stage with a full stomach. At four, we went over to the Civic Center for a sound check. This, too, we were aware, would be our last.

We felt it with the guys in the band. That day was finally here and everyone was talking a little faster and laughing a little louder and seemingly trying not to notice that proverbial elephant in the room. We ran a few songs for levels, a couple for tempo, and even one or two we weren't even planning on singing because somebody in the band just wanted to play it one more time. Then we left and were whisked back to the hotel for a shower and shave and one last hotel room. I was glad Debbie was with me. It made that final walk to the bus with my luggage a little less severe. Other family began to join us and then as we were about to pull out, Jimmy Dean and his wife, Donna, arrived to follow us back over to the arena. The march was on.

Six months ago almost to the day, the tickets had gone on sale for this final concert and it sold out in one hour and 27 minutes. Fans had been holding their breaths for this night nearly as long as we had. We dressed in the back aisle of the bus in front of our individual closets, talking and laughing as usual. Nothing seemed much different except when we all four entered the lounge, Jimmy Dean was sitting on the sofa waiting on us. We had invited him, old friend that he is, to introduce us for the last time. We continued our pre-show ritual by singing, a capella, an old hymn to warm up our voices just before we went on. Every night it would be a different one—"Rock of Ages," "Revive Us Again," "Precious Memories." And then the final thing before we exited the bus was always a prayer. This had been standard procedure since we were kids back home singing on weekends for two dollars a night. We always had a prayer and we took turns each night. We have been joined by some wonderful people in our group prayers throughout the years. Even when we did our TV series in the 90s, that would be the last thing we did before we left the dressing room. We've had James Blackwood join us. Jake Hess. Vestal Goodman. And until you had heard that lady pray, you had no idea what heaven would be like. Even years before that, we had been joined by Johnny Cash and Carl Perkins and June Carter and others. And tonight, for the last one, Jimmy Dean joined us. And then it was "Amen" and out the door and people were snapping pictures and someone was asking, "Are you ready?" and someone else was saying, "Would you sign this?" And suddenly in my head all the music stopped and everything went into slow motion and I could only hear the silence. And I could only see my Brothers as I had seen them so many times before. So many times in the last 38 years I had caught myself standing on the stage while one of them sang a solo and seeing them not as the audience was seeing them, but seeing them as *I* knew them. Seeing Phil, standing there in that shiny suit and starched shirt, and yet I was visualizing a skinny little blonde-haired, barefooted boy who used to hang around our house because he and Harold were best friends. Then I'd look over and see Lew with the guitar around his neck and I'd see the boy Harold brought home with him in grade school who had just moved to town and liked to play the mandolin. Or I'd see Jimmy hitting the high note and remember the first day he came to us, nervous and hungry to do something with his talent. And then I'd see Harold in the spotlight and watch him control the crowd and think to myself, "This is the guy I used to share a room with growing up? This is the big brother who taught me everything I know about girls and softball and life in general?" And I'd say to myself, "How did all these kids get up here on stage? This can't be. We're just a bunch of boys who grew up together, played ball together, double-dated and went to church and the movies together. We're nothing special. How did this happen to us and who are these men that everybody is applauding and clamoring for?"

And that was what was in my head just before I heard someone read a telegram of congratulations from the stage signed "George and Laura Bush." That was my final thought just before I heard "Ladies and Gentlemen, the Statler Brothers" for the last time. That was what was rushing through my mind as I followed the other three on the stage and into the lights that night…"Where are those kids and how did they get to be these men and why is everybody standing and clapping?"

Chapter Two

---◆---

Knock-knock jokes
Who's there?
Dewey
Dewey who?
Dewey remember these, yes we do,
Ah, do we, do we remember these
—Harold Reid, Don Reid and Larry Lee
"Do You Remember These?"

— Harold —

The 1950s were a magical time. America felt safe with Eisenhower, who was like everybody's favorite uncle and enchanted with Elvis, who was everybody's black sheep cousin. We were a bunch of small-town Virginia boys who didn't know what a great adventure we were about to have. We didn't know that many successful years later we would be responsible for declaring to nostalgia fans all over the world that the 50s was the greatest decade of the 20th century. We couldn't have known that back then. What lay ahead was more than we had any right to expect or enough imagination to dream about.

Today we would say we came from a working, middle class. Back then labels weren't so important. We were friends. No. We were buddies. We played ball, picked guitar, sang in the choir and went to church on Sundays. That's what Joe McDorman was going to do that first summer Sunday night in June of '55. The Lyndhurst Methodist Church needed some special music.

They had no idea how special it was going to be. Especially for us.

<u>Joe called Lew</u>. Lew DeWitt was a classmate of Joe's. Lew played guitar and sang all the harmony you'd ever want from a 17-year-old tenor.

<u>Lew called Harold</u>. When Lew called me I thought it was a great idea except even I knew you needed another part. I didn't know what you called it, but I knew we had to have it. My voice had changed almost overnight and I had been singing in the school choir for almost two years. It wasn't pretty, but it was loud.

<u>I called Phil</u>. Phil was and always has been my best friend. He comes from a musical family. Like I said, I knew we needed some musical space filled in to make a quartet and Phil can fill in all the space that's left. And that, my friends, is an understatement.

It was Sunday afternoon and we needed that special music by 7:30. So us "boys" (as we would affectionately be called for years), came up with everybody's favorite gospel song, "A Little Talk With Jesus." Now as any gospel music expert worth his double-breasted suit will tell you, if your tenor is high enough and your bass is low enough, you've got a winner. I won't say it was good, but being a 15-year-old bass singer, I will say we got their attention. Our reviews from the congregation ranged from "wonderful" to "terrific." And they made the mistake of inviting us back. Folks, that's all it took. We went into rehearsal like an old Broadway show with a new angel.

All summer we played any church that would leave the door unlocked. We practiced indoors, outdoors, in the car, and on the run. We didn't just have a temperature; we were running a fever. It was a summer of yearning, learning and planning. We figured anything that was this much fun must be against the law. So we sang and dreamed and dreamed and sang.

If this idea was going to work, we had to call it something. That's not as easy as it sounds. All the good names like The Statesmen, The Four Lads, or the Ames Brothers were already spoken for or in this case, sung for. Within a couple of weeks' time, we were watching TV, between working up new songs, when a show titled *Four Star Theater* was rolling the closing credits. I said, "What a great name for a group." Everyone agreed. Look out world, here comes the Four Star Quartet.

Then it happened. The fall of that year we entered a small talent contest at a local school (we would later own). We won first place! If there was any doubt what we wanted to do forever, that did it. We were hooked. Joe, Lew, Phil and I played anywhere anyone would listen; sometimes with guitar, sometimes a cappella. In early 1956 we improved our sound and asked an exceptional piano player to join us. It wasn't like the great gospel quartets we admired so much. We had to settle for a girl! Peggy Smiley was the best the Shenandoah Valley had to offer. It was said that Peggy had been playing so long and so well that she had to pay income tax before she graduated from high school. That was a pretty good recommendation. We had practically grown up with her and knew there was none better. She could listen to a Blackwood Brothers record and sit right down and play a piano break just like Jackie Marshall.

Peggy would come to rehearsal smiling and leave laughing and make everyone feel special just being with her. I guess that's what caused our first show-biz complication. Lew wound up with a pretty big crush on her. Peggy, in her jolly way, took him off, talked him out of love and made him like her for it. She was very special. Peggy would soon leave, become engaged and get married. Fifty plus years later, she's still happy and still a great friend. And she can still make a piano talk.

It was back to the four of us. We had a radio station in the area that employed a North Carolina quartet called The Friendly Four. They would do about two live radio shows per day on WSVA in Harrisonburg and then go out and play concerts on weekends. One weekend they were promoting a 'sing' with several other groups in Petersburg, West Virginia. Now, we were not known or important enough to get invited to anything of that scale, but we got up on Saturday, dressed alike in our stage outfits, drove 150 miles to

Petersburg and stopped to explain that we were returning from a singing engagement of our own and, yes, we would be glad to do a number. We did. Sometimes a quartet's just gotta do what a quartet's gotta do.

Singing came to be the top priority in our lives. In fact, in February 1957 I had a date with a 15-year-old girl and took her on our first date to hear us sing. Now it wasn't very fancy but I guess it was the right thing to do. Her name was Brenda Armstrong and it's 50 years later and we're still on that same date after five kids and thousands more concerts.

It would be worth noting here that we now had things like full-time jobs. Boy, they can really get in the way sometimes. Joe was working for a painting company; Phil and I were working in a men's clothing store; and Lew was driving a cab. We weren't hungry, but we sure weren't satisfied.

We got wind of an East Coast talent show in Frederick, Maryland, over Labor Day weekend. Now let me brag a little here. We had entered and won several talent shows by this time. So when we heard there were $500 and musical opportunities involved, we started asking for the time off from work. Mr. Wright, who owned the store where Phil and I worked said, "Yes," we could go, but, "don't come back." We went. We came in fourth. We were beat out by a dog act, a pretty girl, and a kid duet. So what you've always heard about never going on stage with kids or dogs is true. I'll let you decide about pretty girls.

Anyway, we came back on Monday morning and Mr. Wright was standing on the sidewalk asking for the store keys. (Oh yeah, I forgot to tell you, I was the assistant manager.) So Phil and I were unemployed. Joe convinced his boss he had been working all weekend and the cab company didn't even miss Lew. What could have been our big break might have been the beginning of our break-up. We were four friends who had a dream but not a goal. Joe and Phil accepted jobs that took them to Florida. Then Lew took a job in Baltimore. I was a pretty lonely boy 'cause one man "ain't no quartet." Sometimes four-part harmony is more than an experience. It's an addiction.

★ ★ ★ ★

Phil Balsley. The experts say that 1939 was Hollywood's golden year. It certainly was for Phil and me. We were born that August, 13 days and two miles apart. Our mothers were church friends and were connected that way the rest of their lives so it wasn't surprising that Phil and I were destined to be best friends. I have memories of Phil as far back as Kindergarten Sunday School Class. He is a perfect gentleman with his mother's nature and his father's looks. He got a double dip of musical talent. His dad sang any part that appealed to his mood and his mom played piano and sang the sweetest alto this side of The Chuck Wagon Gang. Phil did not realize then or now the extent of his abilities. Lew used to tell him that he should be singing tenor. He probably would have if we hadn't been blessed with two great tenors like Lew and Jimmy.

Phil is easy to get along with but not easy to explain. Once in our teenage years we were sitting in his room with a problem we thought was insurmountable. We both had dates; we had permission to use his dad's car; but we had a total of two dollars between us. Now two dollars at that time would get you 10 gallons of gas, but that doesn't buy movie tickets or popcorn. After a while, I walked over to Phil's dresser where his wallet laid and picked it up for no particular reason because he'd already told me how broke he was. I turned around and said, "Phil, there's eight dollars in your billfold." He said, "Oh, I know. I wasn't counting that."

I want you to understand that the way I remember it we made two girls very happy that night. What I don't understand is why he has kept our books for 45 years. I guess we figured we would always have a little more than he told us about.

Phil was away from home for the second time. The first time he had gone to D.C. to work for the FBI. He wasn't exactly an agent but he did ride on the elevator one time with J. Edgar Hoover. That position only lasted a few months. This time he had a construction job in Florida. He was living with the family he worked for and he'd bought a '53 Studebaker.

Now even I know that a man who was run out of Washington by J. Edgar, then runs away from home again, lives with strangers and buys a Studebaker is not rational, so I talked him into coming home for a visit. He said okay but our buddy, Joe, was staying in Florida. He had a job with the same family and construction company with one more complication. He was in love and was going to get married. Now I'll be honest with you. Stuff like this can mess up a singing group. Love is fine, but after all, Joe was a pretty good lead singer.

Phil came home. It took me two days to talk him into staying. He never went back to say good-bye to the family or the Studebaker. The family parked it in the front yard with the keys in it. Finally they moved and as far as we know, that Studebaker is still there. So much for Grand Theft Auto. Of course, I was willing to give up Phil's car for a great baritone. It was late winter 1960 and I had half a quartet. Things were about to change.

★ ★ ★ ★

Lew DeWitt. Lew was the first to tell the world that he never liked the idea of working 9 to 5. Singing and picking were lots more fun.

Like the time in high school when I was working weekends at a grocery store. It was very busy and there was lots of work bagging and stocking shelves. The other part-time boy confided to me that this was his last week. Lew had been telling me how desperately he wanted a job, so I went to my boss and begged him to hire Lew. Finally he told Lew he could start to work on Thursday afternoon. Lew said, "Oh, I can't do it right away. I'd like to take that first weekend off." So I worked Thursday, Friday and Saturday alone. It was the last time I acted as a job broker.

Anyway, in the spring of '60, Lew was in Baltimore trying to keep from getting a job while looking to get some guitar experience playing clubs. I knew the ratio of clubs to guitar players and also knew Lew probably wouldn't be bagging groceries for a living, so it didn't take much to talk him into coming home to the Shenandoah Valley. I was starting to feel better. I had a baritone, a tenor on the way, my desire to sing, and an idea.

★ ★ ★ ★

Don Reid. It was a "right under your nose" situation. My little brother, Don, had come along in 1945 and changed my life forever. I had an older sister and didn't really figure I had any real use for a baby brother. After all, he just took up a lot of my mother's time and as far as I could tell didn't know Roy Rogers from Roy Acuff. I finally decided if he was going to stay, I'd better take him under my wing and teach him about life, love and larceny.

It took me a long time to realize he was learning a lot faster than I was teaching. I still remember when I was about 13 years old I spent at least two weeks spitting down the front of my shirt trying to whistle through my teeth. Don, who was about 7, asked, "Is this what you're trying to do?" At this point, I swear to the Lord, he whistled louder and better than I had ever in the whole 14 days. That's the way he is. If he ain't good the first time, he'll woodshed till he can do anything he set out to do.

I could tell you how I started out to teach him to write a song, but that's a little too embarrassing being as how he's written some of the greatest songs I've ever heard. I tell you all this because I know now it was all meant to be. At this time in his life he had spent more time sitting at the piano playing than standing in the bathroom shaving. He was a natural.

So Phil and Lew and I started rehearsing with my little brother. And there was a sound we had never heard. There was an energy we had never felt. This was special.

Finally we had an appearance scheduled. We walked on the stage, sang two songs and stepped back. We three looked at Don and I said, "Take it." And he did. He stepped to the mike and nailed down the job of master of ceremonies.

He was fourteen years old.

He was good.

The rest is history.

★ ★ ★ ★

We saw this as a brand new start, so a new name would make it complete. We came up with The Kingsmen. (Get it? Gospel quartet. Kingsmen?) It sounded good to us so we went to work to try and live up to our own expectations. The day jobs were a burden because now three of us had wives and children. Don was in high school and then college, so we worked around impossible schedules and honest obligations.

We landed a 15-minute gospel program on WSIG Mt. Jackson radio. We drove the 50 miles north each Wednesday night to record it, and they would broadcast it back south each Sunday morning. We were on the air!

We would go by our hometown station, WTON, and guest with life-long friend Ray Houser. Ray was a cum laude graduate of the old school of broadcasting. He would just sit down at a piano and do a 30-minute show on the spot. We had some great times. Fun was up but profits were down so we had to make some business decisions. We were in a small market where entertainment was concerned. We couldn't make the market larger so we decided to make ourselves bigger and more versatile. We wrote and developed three different concepts for what we saw as the three different concert opportunities in our area. We had a country show complete with all country songs and impressions that paid tribute to Ferlin Husky, Gene Autry, Roy and Dale and, of course, The Sons of the Pioneers. We used this one at grand openings, festivals or country music parks. We were regulars at Oak Leaf Park near Luray, VA, for several seasons. It was the first time we would come in contact with stars like Buck Owens, the Louvin Brothers, Leroy Van Dyke, and Loretta Lynn. Lots of fun and a little money, too.

We also had a large convention hotel in our area that would recommend us for their out-of-town crowds. If they were a little more 'tuned-in' to the popular music of the day, we had that, too. This show consisted of more urban tunes like "Autumn Leaves" and our impersonations of Bing Crosby, Dean Martin, Ernie Ford, The Ink Spots, and even the McGuire Sisters. We did these during the week and on Saturday nights and we still had our complete gospel program for Sundays. We did the same songs for the morning or evening church services. You could sing them a little faster and louder on Sunday nights. I don't know why that is, but it's true.

Bouncing around like that, we finally worked our way to a television show on Channel 7 in Roanoke. Again, we would tape once a week and race back home for a little shut-eye and be at work by 8:30 the next morning. We were growing and our tour circle became larger and larger. As word spread, we were not just playing in and around Virginia but outside the state. All this was great except for one thing. You still had to be back by 8:30 for work.

Then out of the blue we were notified by Channel 7 that we were getting mail at the station that was not ours. It seems there was another Channel 7 just over in North Carolina and also another Kingsmen Quartet. (No wonder that name had sounded so good to us.) Gospel fans everywhere are familiar with Eldridge Fox and the great Kingsmen from Asheville, NC, and we were over-lapping not only in mail but in TV signals. We were the upstarts so we started looking for a new moniker. When we have the scent, it doesn't take us long to pick up a trail. Within a very short period of time we were sitting in a room, again rehearsing, and on a table was a box of Statler tissues. We all looked at each other and agreed it was a good, solid name and as far as we knew no one had a group by that name; maybe a hotel, but not a singing group. Look out world, here come the Statler Brothers!

Chapter Three

It started March of sixty-four, many years ago
We were hired by Johnny Cash to open up his show
Four boys, a worn-out Cadillac with a road map on the dash
For the next eight and one-half years we got paid by Cash
— Harold Reid and Don Reid
"We Got Paid By Cash"

— Don —

Sometime in the mid-summer of '63, we hooked up with a local promoter and agent from the Roanoke area, Carlton Haney, who claimed he knew Johnny Cash and could get us an introduction and interview with him. He said, "Only three artists have ever packaged their own shows: Hank Williams, Elvis, and Johnny Cash. Hank's dead and Elvis has the Jordanaires, so let's go meet Johnny."

As luck and providence would have it, John was playing the fair in Roanoke the next month, so off we went and caught his show. After the performance Carlton took us backstage and we were presented to this long, skinny, sweat-soaked man dressed in a black suit and open-neck white shirt who sort of glared and studied us more than greeted us. We each shook his hand and when it came Harold's turn he said to him, "We have a group I'd like for you to hear sometime."

Shocking all of us, John said, in what would become a familiar, low and growling voice to us in the near-future, "I'd like to. I'm going to be at Berryville Sunday. You know where that is?" We all shook our heads in the

17

direction of 'yes' even though we had no idea where or what he was talking about. "Come up there and I'll put you on the show." And that was it. That was our introduction and our interview.

Berryville turned out to be a little village in Virginia about a hundred miles from our hometown that had a country music park that was typical in the South and Midwest in those days. The park consisted of an outdoor stage along a little river with wooden benches and acres for campers and Sunday tailgaters. It still stands there today pretty much as it was then, but that Sunday afternoon it was about to be a part of history in more ways than one. The first way was that a record crowd was overflowing the grounds and folks were wading in the river to get a look at the man they had all come to see. We were some of those expectant and waiting people even though we were behind the stage in full suited attire. And we waited well past show time before we finally saw a small dust bubble in the distance coming from a car that everyone was saying Johnny was in. As it got closer and closer and then finally there, out he stepped, clad just as he had been two days ago at the fair and his arrival was a sign the show could begin. His bass player, Marshall Grant, came to us and said we were to open the show. He suggested we do about fifteen minutes so Johnny could see what our act consisted of. The people were getting restless and anxious to see the man they'd paid to hear and were yelping for "Johnny! Johnny! Johnny!"

But on we went and to our collective surprise, we looked over during our first song and saw that John had brought a chair out to the side of the stage and was sitting there in full-view of the audience, watching us. Now it's hard enough to keep the attention of a crowd who is waiting for the head-liner (ask anyone who ever opened for the Beatles or Sinatra) but when that superstar is sitting there for all the world to see, distraction does not even begin to describe the havoc that could have ensued and disrupted our 'audition.' But undaunted and having no choice, we plowed right through every song and joke and routine that we could squeeze into twenty minutes (yeah,

I know Marshall said fifteen, but then you always take what you need and apologize later), and that hot and tired crowd loved it! They were on their feet and so was John.

We came off to handshakes and compliments and back pats that sent us into the promise of all of the immediate good things that we knew were going to happen. In a matter of minutes someone was introducing John and he was on the stage and our heads were swimming into dreams as we changed clothes and waited impatiently for him at the stage door.

He sang his last encore and came down the steps toward us and while that multitude of fans was still in a frenzy of applause and a fever of wanting more, the Man in Black got in the back seat of his waiting car and that same bubble of dust that brought him down that dirt road took him away again. Our audition was over. And maybe even our career.

We played a little church in the area that same night for a freewill offering as was our usual Sunday night fare and told, between songs, the experience we had had that day. All the people in the congregation were happy for our possibilities even if our own expectations were at a low ebb. But what I recall most about that evening song service, at what I think was the Toms Brook Methodist Church, was that the minister, in his benediction, after we finished singing, prayed for our success and asked each member to do the same when they went home. I only wish I remembered his name. Many times through the years I have wanted to thank him for his faith and his kindness. And some day I will.

★ ★ ★ ★

Months went by with no word from anybody on anything. More months and no call from Carlton Haney or Cash and we were boiling in our youthful ambitions. Harold got on the phone and by charm and crook came up with John's home phone number in Casita Springs, California. His wife,

Vivian, who told us later she remembered the call, confided in him, for some odd reason, that John was in New York doing a TV show called *HULLA-BALOO*. A few calls to Information got him the studio number and he wound up talking to John's agent, Saul Holiff. That contact proved effective many weeks later when Holiff called back and asked if we would like to do a concert with John in Canton, Ohio, on March 8, 1964. Our answer was unanimous and fervent. But here is what we were faced with. Harold and Phil were both married with two children each and Lew was married with one. I was the only one who was single with virtually no risks at all, and yet we were all four determined to either stare down our fate or give up our dream. And it would never be a better time than right then. So they all three quit their day-jobs and I quit business school and we kissed the families goodbye, packed a little homemade trailer that Phil's dad had built for us, full of most all the clothes we had and planned a northwest trip for Ohio. All we had been promised was one date on March 8, but we decided among ourselves that after that show we would head either to New York or Nashville and take whatever singing work we could find.

Less than three days before we were ready to pull out of town in our twelve-year-old Cadillac limo, pulling that sheet-metal trailer, we got another call from Saul Holiff. John wanted to hire us for the entire tour which would last a week and a day. We had never worked eight consecutive days in our lives, so there we went, heading for the big time with Carlton Haney, who was the oddest and strangest little man you can ever imagine, sitting right up between us in the backseat.

We arrived in the early morning, checked into the George Washington Hotel, which is surely gone the way of all flesh by now, and then dressed and went to church, a habit we often practiced throughout our career when our travel schedule would allow. Four Presbyterian-raised boys saying a final prayer at the First Baptist Church of Canton before going to the Memorial Auditorium and getting ready for the most important 2:30 matinee of their lives. It was an all-star show and we met, that first day, some people who would become lifelong friends. On the show was The Duke of Paducah, George Hamilton IV, Sonny James, Bill Anderson, June Carter, and of course, John, who never showed up until it was time for him to go on stage, and therefore no one else on the show knew that we were supposed to perform. The building manager and the entire cast had no idea who we were but they all were so gracious and accommodating and made us feel at least three shades lighter green than we actually were.

Between the matinee and evening shows that day, John and his troupe sat with us in the dressing room and had us sing song after song. Luther Perkins, his guitar player, asked us to sing "How Great Thou Art," which we subsequently did many times for Luther before a show as it was his favorite. John officially told us we were hired as part of his traveling show; we settled on a daily price (which to save my life or his reputation, I can't remember what it was) and then he said to be in Rockford, Illinois, the next night. And then we shook hands. And that was it! No contract. No lawyers. No agents. John said, "People who have to have contracts don't trust one another." How often does that happen? Not very in this business, I assure you. But that's all we had. For eight and a half years—a handshake. What a great way for friends to do business.

He took Carlton Haney off into another room, paid him off with an undetermined amount of cash and a plane ticket home. Haney came out grinning and stopped to offer us greenhorns one last piece of advice. He said to us, just before leaving the theater, "Always order eggs on the road, 'cause nobody can hurt an egg." The man was deep. And he also apparently never ate in some of the places we would eventually eat in on the road because they *can* hurt an egg.

★ ★ ★ ★

We were doing an impression of John in our portion of the show. Harold actually did his voice singing "Ring of Fire" and Phil and Lew and I would do the trumpets with our lips up next to the microphone. It was a great bit and the people loved it; only problem was, so did John. He loved it so much that after the first night he said, "Why don't you all come out on my portion of the show and do those trumpets when I sing 'Ring of Fire?' And while you're out there, we'll do 'The Ballad of a Teenaged Queen.'" So in one fell swoop, on the second night of the tour, we lost a comedy bit for our show and started the tradition of going back out and singing with John on his. This cast-gathering finale grew over the years and eventually included June and the Carter Family and Carl Perkins and whoever else may be traveling with us at the time.

That first week we ate late snacks in June's room after the shows. We sat up and sang in John's room until all hours of the morning. We sang songs in the dressing rooms with Bill Anderson. And when that first week ended the following Sunday night in Davenport, Iowa, we were as happy as we had been the previous Sunday night. We got paid, turned that beat-up Caddy and trailer toward the east, and just as we were about to pull out, John said, "Next tour starts April 2 at the University of Alabama. And then we'll go to Nashville and you'll cut a record on the third."

We drove back home to Virginia that night in alternate moods of silence, glee and suspicion. Could life really be this good?

★ ★ ★ ★

The rest of 1964 was a blur of culture shock, sometimes in slow motion and sometimes so fast we couldn't feel the wind at our backs that was pushing us toward a future we had only dreamed of. We were back on tour every month with the Cash troupe and yes, we did cut our first record that next trip as promised. It was "The Wreck of the Old 97" and even with John blowing the train whistle on it and performing a recitation with us on the flipside, it was a major flop. But with all that was going on around us, we never took time to worry too much about that.

May found us driving across the country and seeing it all for the first time and finally arriving in Hollywood and getting a rather frantic first-hand tour with John driving us around the mystic city in his open-top Jeep with faulty brakes. It was a sight-seeing tour to remember. Having grown up in an East Coast, shoreline state, but having never done much traveling until then, we *saw* and *swam* in the Pacific before we did the Atlantic.

June 1 found us in New York City for the first time and on *The Tonight Show* with Johnny Carson and Lawrence Welk and Woody Allen. We rehearsed in the afternoon, taped at dinner time, and by air time, 11:15 p.m. eastern, we were down in the Village seeing the town. Someone remembered about 11 o'clock that the show was about to start and we began a frenzied search for a TV set. We split up and were running in and out of restaurants and clubs and shops and finally found a store with a small black and white that was closing but was nice enough to let us come in and watch ourselves on our first network appearance.

The cloud we were floating on when we went to bed that night burst and came pouring down on us hard the next morning. There is a Catch-22 when it comes to joining any entertainment union which, by law, you have to be a member of. AFTRA, American Federation of Television and Radio Artists, is what you must belong to in order to sing over the airwaves. Now to become a member, you have to have a job already booked but in order to legally book a job, you have to be a member. Thus the Catch-22 I spoke of. So our representative, Saul Holiff, John's manager, had arranged with NBC for us to do *The Tonight Show* without a union card if we would promise to go over and join the first thing the next morning. John was meeting us at 10 a.m. to make all this happen.

Well, 10 a.m. came and went and we got our first glimpse of how John would drop out of sight mentally and physically from time to time because of his personal demons. He became a different person than we had known. He could lose and gain 20 pounds overnight; he could lose all reasoning powers and manners; and though never harmful to anyone but himself, he could turn life upside down for everyone who cared and worried about him. This was one of those mornings. He stayed locked in his room over at Delmonico's while June was in hers, upset and frightened. We were called over to their hotel and after spending some time with her and telling her how John was going to join us up with AFTRA but now we couldn't because we didn't have the $200 cash, June loaned us the money, we joined the union, came back and spent the day with her. That night the five of us went out to eat at La Scala's and did The Big Town. We rubbed shoulders with next-table neighbors like Tony Bennett and Xavier Cugat and Frankie Avalon and Sam Cooke. It was like these four Virginia boys had died and gone to New York. Each month found us on tour joined by major country music stars of the day: Webb Pierce, Kitty Wells, Tex Ritter, a young Hank Williams, Jr. Hank Jr. was about 15 years old, just a few years younger than me, and he would hide out in our dressing room from his mother, Audrey, whom he called "The Big A," and smoke. Let me hasten to add, tobacco. But the one who stole our hearts from day one, was Tex. He had been a hero of our dad's for years and we had gone to all of his movies as kids and now we were traveling on the same nightly tour and he was everything you ever wanted him to be: lovable, grouchy, gruff, and funny. We'd play draw poker on the rented tour bus and he'd ask for five. Who's going to tell Tex Ritter you can't draw five? We'd eat meals together and one morning at breakfast he stared viciously at Harold, who had just ordered pancakes and smothered them with gravy, and said, "What's wrong with you, boy?" After explaining that this is the way we eat 'em back in Virginia, he'd just shake his head, snort, and pack his pipe and grin that all-knowing grin that was all his. When changing clothes before and after a show, he never, never took off his boots. They would go right through the pants legs with his feet. Many nights between shows he would sit in his shirt and tie, boxer shorts and cowboy boots and smoke his pipe and read the paper.

We became great friends with Tex and his wife, Dorothy, and when we played California, he brought his two young sons, John and Tom, to the shows. We spent a lot of dressing room time with Tex telling stories about the old Western films, Broadway, and early country music. He had been where we wanted to go and we were good listeners.

They eventually moved to Nashville and we saw them even more. And the night our daddy died, Tex was on the radio doing the all-night Opry Star Spotlight show on WSM and he talked about him and dedicated the show to him never knowing that a picture we had gotten him to autograph years ago had hung over Daddy's bed ever since and was still hanging there at that very moment. Lovable, gruff old Tex never lost the ability to be a good human being and an unwavering hero.

★ ★ ★ ★

Maybe the memory that stuck with me most that first year was turning 19 years old on the road. We were playing a fair in Chatham, Ontario, on June 5 and after the show that night, across a hot and dusty backstage field, John and June carried to our door a small plate holding a peanut butter sandwich surrounded by two Mars bars with a match stuck in the bread for a candle. They sang "Happy Birthday" to me between shows and I knew then that I was officially show business trash. And I was loving every minute of it.

★ ★ ★ ★

On June 27 we played the Grand Ole Opry for the first time. And by July 28 we were back in Nashville to record our second record for Columbia.

I had been writing since I was 14 and had a catalog of songs building up by the day. We decided that one of mine, "Your Foolish Game," would be our next release backed by an old hit of John's, "I Still Miss Someone." Now comes the next Catch-22. BMI, Broadcast Music Inc., is an organization that logs and pays the songwriter every time his song gets played on the air. In order to join, you have to have a song recorded and in order to get your song recorded . . . do you see where I'm going here again? So you have to lie to someone for a couple of minutes while you run from the studio to the sign-up office and back.

Anyway, Harold and I had begun to write a few things together and unbeknownst to him I put his name on the song also and got him an application so that we would both be ready for our writing careers. Now I don't advise anyone to go giving away songs or even halves of songs, but when it's your brother at least it's in the family and he would have done the same for me and did many times. And in this case it didn't do all that well anyway. It served its purpose by getting us both signed up and ready for our writing careers, but like the first record, it died coming out of the chute.

Chapter Four

'Cause I love the mountains of Virginia
I run back to her every time I can
'Cause I love the valleys of Virginia
Oh, Virginia, I'm back where I began
— Harold Reid and Don Reid
"Virginia"

— Don —

We got a lot of studio time and recording experience by singing back-up on nearly all of John's albums and singles from the day we began with him. The Carter family on one side of the studio, the Statlers on the other, the Tennessee Three supplemented with some of Nashville's finest situated between us, John in the middle, and you pretty much got the same show you got in concert. And this was the setting for our third and final attempt at cutting a hit record for the Columbia label. But first a little backstory.

A year or so earlier, as a favor to Carlton Haney, the guy who took us to Cash, we had gone to a small recording studio in Roanoke and had sung backup for a girl singer by the name of Shirlee Hunter. She recorded a tune called "The Ballad of Billy Christian" and we fell in love with it. The writer of the song was a DJ there in the area who was trying to get his foot in the door in Nashville and we told him if we ever got the chance that we would record it someday also and he thanked us and we all went our merry ways. Well, Shirlee's record and singing career sadly never got off the ground but we remembered our promise and acted on it the first chance we got. And that first chance was one day during a Johnny Cash recording date when John decided he wanted to take a lunch break right in the middle of a three-hour session, so he put on his coat and walked out leaving a studio full of pickers and singers on the clock and cooling their heels.

Our deal with Columbia had been "three strikes and you're out." In other words, they would give us three attempts to cut a hit and then we were out on our ears or whatever else we may land on. The only reason we got even that deal was because John had insisted on it and threatened them with it. So you can well imagine that we were not their favorite people as no one likes to have anything forced on them. And here we were with two failed attempts under our belts and just waiting for them to book us that third, promised session.

About 30 seconds after the door closed behind John and his pursuit to find a ham and cheese sandwich, the producer, Don Law, came in the studio and looked at us and said, "If you guys want to record, you've got till John gets back from lunch," and turned and walked out. This is how much notice and preparation we had for the record that was going to determine if we left or stayed in the music business.

We immediately taught the musicians "The Ballad of Billy Christian" and recorded it in minutes. Watching the clock, we knew we had to have a 'B' side. Lew had just written a song he had sung to us without even a melody. When he first sang it to us, he had sung it to the tune of another song. Just a couple of weeks before he had put an original melody to it so while he showed the chords to the pickers, Phil and I wrote out the lyrics and Harold tweaked the arrangement. And in a few more minutes we had a complete, two-sided record. And just in time as John was back with a toothpick in his mouth.

The song, of course, was "Flowers on the Wall" and when people ask about our genius of using a banjo and gut-string guitars on a record that eventually became a crossover pop hit for us, we can explain it easily. We used the musicians that were there and available to us; the ones John had called for his session who were sitting there watching the clock tick. The Tennessee Three, a banjo, and a rhythm guitar. If there had been a flugelhorn and an oboe, I guess we would have used that, too. Common people don't do great things. Great things happen to common people.

So "Flowers on the Wall" was to be the flipside, but somewhere out there it got turned over and became the hit that started it all off for us. And "Billy Christian" became the 'B' side. But there's a rose in even this side of the story because as the record went on to sell over a million copies, the writer of the 'B' side, our ole DJ buddy from up in Virginia, made a lot of money and confided in us that he made enough from our record to make the move to Nashville and try his hand at what he always wanted to do: write country songs. And he did. Like nobody before him. I shudder to think where country music would be today without Tom T. Hall.

Thirty years later on our TV series, we had Tom T. on as a guest and did a 15-minute salute to him and some of the great songs he has contributed to the industry that he loves. He sat and watched us rehearse it the day before the show and said, "I appreciate what you're doing, but it's kinda like going to my own funeral."

★ ★ ★ ★

Before "Flowers on the Wall" was released and we got an even bigger taste of success and responsibility, we were made an offer that revealed something about ourselves that even we didn't know. It was a most telling aspect of our personal/professional lives and it had an impact that would last beyond our career and into our retirement. Little did we know that on a bright, sunny, Spring morning on the streets of Hollywood would we be made "an offer we *could* refuse."

The four of us, Harold, Phil, Lew and myself, were having breakfast at the Brown Derby on Vine with Cliffie Stone who was a major force in the country music scene on the West Coast. He had been head of the country division of Capitol Records for years and had the respect of everyone in the industry. He had heard us in concert with the Cash Show and he looked across the table at us that morning and offered us a proposition that most would kill for. He pointed out how successful the Jordanaires were in Nashville singing backup vocals on nearly every recording that came out of the town. This was something we didn't need pointed out as we had met them and had seen first-hand their reign on Music Row. They had made a unique place for themselves and were rolling in the dough, never having to leave town. Cliffie went on to say that L.A. was hot on the heels of Nashville in the country music field with the Bakersfield faction and all the TV and movie soundtracks that were produced daily and noted that there was no group at the time to do all this work. He assured us that he could guarantee us the position of "the Jordanaires of Hollywood." All we'd have to do was move to California and our fate was set. Live the good life in Malibu, drive into L.A. for a few sessions each working day, and be home every night with wife and family. Not a bad prospect for four young guys looking to conquer the world. And we didn't take long to give him an answer. But the answer was even more shocking than the offer.

Each of us is Virginia-born. Each of us had grown up in this small, picturesque town in the heart of the Shenandoah Valley called Staunton. (I know how it's spelled, but it's pronounced Stanton. So many times we have overheard fans at the stage door or outside the bus saying to Security, "We know them. We grew up with them in Stawn-ton." When we heard that, we just laughed to ourselves. It was kind of like 'shibboleth' in the Bible; if you can't say it, you ain't from there.)

From the time we were babes in arms, we went to Sunday School and Vacation Bible School and Sunday morning services at the Olivet Presbyterian Church. We played softball on the diamond that is still there behind the parking lot and we still have the green and white uniforms we wore to prove it. Today Harold and Phil and I are Elders at that same church; singing in the choir, teaching Sunday School, taking up collection. And our kids are there, too. Hey, and even our grandkids.

Three of us went to grade school at Beverley Manor Elementary. It closed down years after we all finished the seventh grade there and sadly became an old dark, empty ghost of its former self, an eyesore and a financial dilemma for the whole town. About twenty-five years after we had all left it in our past, we were riding in a parade one Fourth of July that took us right by the front door. We looked over at it and were touched by the shape it was in: broken windows, weedy yard, cracked playground. So the next day, we went to visit it and within weeks bought it and put the four-building complex into a state of repair that would become our home base of operations for the next twenty years. The old school library would become our conference room. The old cafeteria would become a restaurant. The old gymnasium would become a playground for our kids to play basketball and volleyball and a place for local kids to practice their teams. The stage where the Four Star Quartet won their first talent contest would become our rehearsal stage. And my seventh grade classroom would become my office. Finally, like our teachers had tried to get us to do all those years ago, we were working in these rooms.

I just had a random flashback to my first grade room at this very school. I was six and there was a Spring concert of the combined grades coming up. All the first graders joined together and sang a couple of songs. I still remember the words and the haunting, silly little melodies. My teacher walked up and down the rows of desks and listened as we rehearsed and one morning after we finished, she called me and three other students aside and told us that from now on we shouldn't actually sing but only move our lips. She said she would put us on the back row the night of the performance and no one but us would ever know. And no one ever did until now. I wonder if she ever realized the irony of her actions.

All four of us graduated from Wilson Memorial High School. Different years. (A note to all those fans who have claimed to have gone to school with "all those Statler boys": with the age span, you would have had to have failed at least seven years to achieve that dubious feat.) Our school had history. Not only was it named after Woodrow Wilson, the twenty-eighth president of the United States, who was also born in our hometown (or more accurately we were born in his), but it was built as a hospital in World War II to care for and house wounded soldiers. It was here we learned those first formal musical notes. Harold and Phil were in the choral group and I was in the band—alto sax if you must know. And it was here that all those memories that fed our songs through the years were first born. The Friday night football games, the double-dating, the sock hops, the graduations (Harold's class actually applauded for him when he crossed the stage to get his diploma, and yes, he curtsied and tipped his mortarboard), the people and the cloudy memories that let you sometimes record them in your mind a little sweeter than they actually were.

Our little town of 22,000 has a park with a mile and a half circumference that includes swimming pools, ball fields, playgrounds, tennis courts, a golf course, picnic areas and a bandstand that would bring Norman Rockwell to his knees. Downtown, when we were growing up, there were three movie theaters and just down the road, a drive-in. From the time I could walk, Harold took me to the double feature on Saturday mornings at the Strand to see Roy and Gene and a chapter of whatever serial was playing the circuit at the time. We'd shop at stores run by the owners who knew our parents and dine at lunch counters on 20-cent hot dogs and buy comic books and peanuts at local newsstands.

When we were knocking around as kids, singing wherever they'd give us two dollars and a donut, it was the good folks of Staunton who came up with those donuts. The civic clubs let us sing for their business dinners. Social clubs had us sing for their Christmas parties. Area churches had us in nearly every Sunday night to put on a program for a freewill offering. We often heard our fans around the world say that we had put Staunton, Virginia, on the map. How nice, but nothing could be further from the truth. Staunton, Virginia, put us on the map. They kept us eating and gave us stage after stage where we could try out our songs and get the experience to face bigger and more critical audiences. They gave us encouragement and put our picture in the paper and let us sing on the radio for charity events and patted us on the backs and told us how far they knew we would go. They fathered us and then mothered us and nurtured us until we were ready to take that first flight on our own. Staunton, if there is anyway we can ever repay you, just let us know.

So, thanks but no thanks, Cliffie. You're a good man for making the offer, but we've got a place to live.

Chapter Five

He wonders is it worth it all, the money and the lights
He'd give it all up gladly to just be home tonight
Then applause breaks his train of thought, the spot has him embraced
And the tears and the sweat melt together in his face
— Don Reid
"The Star"

— Harold —

I know you're wondering along about here, "is this book gonna tell us some Johnny Cash stories?" The answer is yes. We have about ten thousand. Some good; some not so good. I'll tell you a few and I'll tell you why it's okay to share them. These are some things that happened between John and us. Months or even years later we would laugh about them with him, so I know it's alright with him for me to tell you. You see, I have some guidelines. Nothing that would embarrass him or make him look bad, because he was our number one supporter and he put us where we always wanted to be. And most important, we loved and respected him. Here goes!

Late 60s. Somewhere in Florida. Two shows. 7 & 9. We played the first show to a packed house. Everything was fine. John comes into our dressing room and asks to borrow our brand new Cadillac touring car. We gave him the keys and never saw him again that night. The second show came and went without the star. After June went on and we followed, Marshall Grant, one of the Tennessee Three and major domo of the troupe, announced to the crowd their money would be refunded. So much for the performance.

We had a star and a car missing.

We spread out to search for him and got back to the hotel about 3 a.m. to find John in his room sound asleep. We found our car about six blocks from the hotel. The back of the seats had been neatly cut several times with what appeared to be a sharp knife and the ash trays were full of cigar stubs. We didn't ask and he didn't say. After all, the car ran fine and we didn't worry about a little cigar smoke. We were just trying to set the world on fire.

Now when things like this would happen, you wouldn't know if John was fighting himself, one of his demons, or he'd just had a fight with June. Sometimes he didn't even know. It certainly caused you to live on the edge. We tried always to be amused but never surprised. Like the night we packed up and left home for a two-week tour. I was driving, we had the radio on and were just starting through Rainelle, West Virginia, heading for the Midwest when the news was reported that country singer Johnny Cash had left the scene of an accident in Nashville after borrowing a friend's car and hitting a telephone pole. I didn't even hit the brake or say a word. I just turned left into a service station, circled around the driveway and headed back to Staunton. It was ten miles before we quit laughing and we were right. The tour was cancelled before we got home. It was only a little inconvenient for us. John always took the hardest hits. We learned a lot from him. We learned a lot of things not to do.

★ ★ ★ ★

There was one cold fall night and day and night we drove to Davenport, Iowa, to begin a tour. We would stop periodically and phone for updates on John's status. (This was before cell phones but boy, they sure would have been handy.) We were almost there when Lew said a famous line from the back-seat that we would laugh about for years. He said, "It's better to drive to Davenport and not do a show than to drive to Davenport and have to do a show." Well, this time we did a show even though John was nowhere to be found. Someone contacted Roger Miller and he came out to fill in. Just the Statlers and Roger. We finished the concert, went back to the hotel, sat up all night with Roger, laughing and telling lies, then jumped in the car and drove back to Virginia. It was one of those times that we kept the promoter from suing John. It was a repayment to the Man in Black. The stomachaches we had from laughing all night with Miller—that's worth a million bucks.

★ ★ ★ ★

Any successful man is leery of what people want from him. That's natural. John was no exception. He didn't even find it unusual when the old car we were driving in those first months let us down in Kansas City and we had to go to him to borrow $350. What he did find unusual was that we went to him the following month and handed him an envelope with $350 inside. He threw it on the floor and said, "You guys are getting ready to leave me, aren't you?" We assured him that all we intended was to say thanks and pay back the money. It took about an hour, but he finally came over to us and said, "I'm sorry. I didn't understand. You see no one has ever paid back money I've loaned them before."

He had already given us a career boost that was unheard of in our business. It took him a while to understand our gratitude. It took us years to understand his reservation.

★ ★ ★ ★

It's not easy to headline the Johnny Cash show; even Johnny knew that. It was a big job and a big show. Carl Perkins, The Carter Family, The Tennessee Three, The Statlers and The Man. We were all in the Midwest for a 10-day tour. Well, almost all of us. It seems John never got there, so we had a meeting with the promoter who promised if we would perform sans the star, he could refund at a minimum and save a "no-show" law suit. We all agreed, so for five days Carl would open, then the Carters and June would go till intermission. Then we would close the show, the promoter would then come out and announce he would refund anyone their money if they hadn't had a good time. At the last minute he would let them know that Johnny couldn't be there. That's what you call intimidating an audience. Some wanted refunds, but not very many. So we packed up and moved on to the next town.

Next night, same routine. Pack up and move on. We had this thing under control until the sixth night when a telegram arrived from John who was angry over us all going on with the show without him even though we were doing it to protect him. It said for all of us to leave the tour immediately and be in Nashville on Saturday night to perform with him on the Grand Ole Opry. It went on to say that anyone who wasn't at the Opry could consider themselves fired. We, the whole troupe, stuck together and continued the tour.

The next day he showed up in Kansas City and we all did three shows on a Sunday afternoon. He was in a great mood and it was never mentioned again. It was a little rough for a while but like I said earlier, it's not easy to headline the Johnny Cash Show.

— Don —

And then there were the times when we were in union with John in his disappearance act instead of being some of the victims. Once he was hiding from Columbia Records and Vivian (his wife) and June and Lord knows who else and we hid him out in a little cabin in the woods up near home for about four days and nights. He cooked all of his own meals, made biscuits and gravy and left a mess that an army of Dutch maids couldn't have cleaned up in a year. We took him out at nights and shot pool with him and rode him around and covered for him when the hounds of Nashville got on his trail and then finally saw him back safely to Music City.

Whenever any of the Tennessee Three, John's band, had to be away for whatever reason, one of us would fill in for them. Luther Perkins had to miss a date once and Lew played guitar. Marshall Grant raced boats and sometimes would miss a show and I would play bass. When W.S. Holland was gone, Harold would play the drums. This situation perfectly portrays John's sense of humor because the first night that Harold was about to go on for W.S., John asked Harold if he was okay with everything. (There were never, never any rehearsals.) Harold said, "Yeah, but I sure would appreciate it if you didn't do "Rock Island Line." John said, "I understand completely, no problem."

"Rock Island Line" is an old folk song and John's arrangement was a rather complex rhythm piece that changed tempos about five different times and kept getting faster and faster. He usually did it as about the fourth or fifth song and Harold was relieved to know he wouldn't have to face that one the first night. But, of course, after the first song, John turned to the band and with that little boy grin on his face yelled out to them, "Rock Island Line!" And they were off. It never mattered to him how it came off; he just enjoyed the mischievousness of it all.

Don't know if this would qualify as a 'John story' or a 'Harold story,' maybe both, but it sure was funny. John had a well-admitted habit of calling people in the middle of the night. We all had gotten those late a.m. calls in our hotel rooms and when you were home in the comfort of your own bed, you were not exempt either. He contended that people would remember a call more readily if they're awakened out of a dead sleep than they might if it was, say, two o'clock in the afternoon. And I guess I agree, but it doesn't always work. He would call at any hour and say, "Be in Nashville in the morning for a record session" or "be in New York tomorrow for a TV show" and we were all there...usually. But once after a long and arduous tour, he called Harold, at home, out of bed, at 4 a.m. and said, "I want you all to be in L.A. tomorrow night," and Harold said, "No." John said, "Why," and Harold said, "Because it's too damn far," and hung up. The entire troupe, including John, laughed about this for years.

John was the most unique human being I have ever known. Whether he was doing a war dance with Indian tribes after a concert (which he did), whether he was drawing modern art and hanging them on the seats of airplanes on commercial flights (which he did), or dry shaving in the backseat of a moving vehicle and throwing the razor blades out the window (which he did), he was doing it all from natural instincts and not for attention. This is what made him such a one-of-a-kind human being who was lovable and cherished by fans, friends and family. Through it all he was an artist who understood his art even when others didn't. He gave me the best advice as a songwriter I ever received. Once when I was having trouble with a verse I was writing, I asked his advice and instead of giving me a long involved lecture on technique, he modestly said, "The best way to say anything is to just say it." I carried that simple advice with me through every song I ever wrote.

— Harold —

John swore that his middle initial was just 'R' and nothing more. The only thing I can tell you about that is that one California afternoon, we four went to the Casitas Springs Post Office with him and I spotted a tax bill that was addressed to John Rand Cash. He swore he'd never heard that before, but it would take on a special meaning for years to come when all of us who were closest to him would call him J.R.

So J.R. had invited us to his home in western California for a weekend. He had a beautiful dining room table that he had beaten with a large log chain to make it look old. He butchered a goat in the corner of his office so he could barbeque it for us. We made that trip to the post office with him in a Jeep he was driving that had everything on it but brakes. He took us to downtown Los Angeles to a great music store that he recommended. When we got out to go inside, he said he would pick us up in a few minutes. We didn't see him for another 36 hours. It's the kind of weekend you never forget and I don't have to tell you he's the kind of person that stands out in your memory.

With all these things said, I think I'm ready to choose my favorite memory of the Man in Black. He had a lot of heart and he had a lot of soul. Back then we all talked about how much 'soul' someone might have. 'Soul' is simply the ability to convey how strongly you feel about something to someone else.

John and June had just bought a beautiful home on the lake just outside of Nashville. It was literally built into the side of a rock wall and suited them to a tee. It was impressive but there were no furnishings in it of any kind. John called and asked if we could meet him and June there on a Sunday evening before leaving on a tour Monday morning. They showed us through their very large, very beautiful but very empty house. When we got back to the kitchen, they told us why they wanted us to be the first to visit. John said he wanted our blessing. We told him that was automatic. He asked if we would sing "How Great Thou Art" to assure their home would be happy. So in the twilight, the four of us blessed John and June's home. I don't think I've ever enjoyed singing it more than when their rooms echoed our harmony.

On second thought, I was wrong by calling it an empty house. It was anything but empty that long-ago evening as the sun was going down over Old Hickory Lake. I believe we did a good job because it sure felt like a happy home to us.

★ ★ ★ ★

P.S. This is one of those stories that makes a perfect circle. Here's the happy ending. A few years later, Brenda and I had just finished renovation on a 150-year-old farm house in Staunton. We didn't move in because it was time again to celebrate the Fourth of July. This was 1973 and John and June were our guests for Happy Birthday U.S.A. We did the show on Wednesday night and on Thursday John, June, the Tennessee Three plus all the Statler families had a picnic in our house with not one stick of furniture. We ate on the patio and sat on the floor. Everyone thought it was great.

So John, June and my Brothers blessed our little farm. You see, anyone can have a dinner party, but only real friends can have a picnic in an empty house. It makes mine a happy home. Thanks guys.

Chapter Six

And we wouldn't trade it all
For the world and all its gold
It's the past that makes the future worth living
— Don Reid
"We"

— Harold —

Anytime you start a new business, you need money. You need other stuff, too, but whether it's show business or shoe business, you better have a little folding green. Now I may be giving away a secret here, but you can bet any act that travels, entertains and records music wants you to drop by their concessions table so they can pay the motel, put fuel in the bus and order a bad sandwich from room service. In other words, it helps pay expenses. It's always been that way.

It was no different when we started our touring career. We knew you should keep the profits up and the expenses down. If you sell your records and pictures at a concert auditorium, the building takes a percentage of your sales. The state takes a percentage of your sales and the city takes a percentage of your sales. Sometimes you don't have a very good percentage left for yourself.

We had already learned this that cold fall night in 1964 when we were asked by the officials at the Canadian border if we had anything to declare. We also knew if you declared your merchandise, they would get their percentage. So we said, "No, I don't think we do." You see they call this a duty tax. It's their duty to ask for it. It's our duty to try to avoid paying it.

We got to the arena that night and the audience liked us well enough to come to the edge of the stage at intermission to buy records and get autographs. We were doing a brisk business, as they say, when a gentleman says to me, "May I see you a moment?" I said, "Yes, sir, I'll get to you as quick as I can." Then I dived back into the retail sales and scribbled signatures.

He approached me the second time and when he saw that he wasn't exactly next in my line, he said, "Sir, I'm with the Royal Canadian Mounted Police." Now that put him next in line. He asked very politely about our sales; what had or had not been declared and informed us that we would be leaving with him immediately after the show. We said, "Yes, sir." We had listened to enough old time radio to know you don't argue with Sgt. Preston.

We arrived at the judge's chambers and were told we were in a wee bit of trouble. I think it's fair to tell you here that we hadn't done anything that hundreds of other acts had not done before. But it seems the northern authorities decided this would be as good a time as any to crack down on some of these 'hillbilly' entertainers. The judge explained that our case would be heard in court the next morning and demanded to know who the merchandise belonged to. If it was all four of us then we would all spend the night in jail. I spoke up and said it all belonged to me, so I got the honor of sleeping on a metal bed all by myself.

To say the least, it was an experience. To say the most, it was jail time.

The next morning they came down to my cell and marched me out and up the stairs to the courtroom with about eight of the dirtiest and meanest looking criminals I'd ever seen. Without bragging I can tell you I was the cleanest and most innocent looking one there. Sitting on the front row were my three Brothers, Phil, Lew and Don, along with our old dependable friend, Marshall Grant of the Tennessee Three. I was called between burglars and wife-beaters and the judge handed down the fine. We had made just enough the night before to get me out of jail. The rest of the story is this: we traveled and toured many times in Canada over the years and when a border official would ask, "Anything to declare?" we handed him a list with everything counted down to the last 8x10 picture. Like I've always said, "I'm just ugly, I ain't stupid."

★ ★ ★ ★

We observed years later that when we were on the road, traveling together, we could recall almost every day or every place we'd ever been if just one of us remembered a small detail. It might be something that happened during the show or in the parking lot. It might even be a hotel desk clerk from those very lean years that caught four of us sneaking up the back stairs when only one of us had checked in. We paid him for the other three. After all, we never set out to be dishonest; just economical.

Some memories are small and almost forgotten while others will live as long as we will. We were in England in the spring of 1966 starting a full-blown European tour. This was our first across-the-ocean experience. We found out a lot about ourselves and the rest of the world. We found a hotel in Scotland that had one bathroom at the end of each hall. We found heated towel racks in Germany. We found American movies but couldn't find plain old American popcorn. (For me it's an essential item.) We went to Piccadilly Circus and Carnaby Street. We saw Big Ben and Buckingham Palace and thought how far away it was from Virginia.

We had a night off on May 21 and it turned out to be one of those memorable times. There was at least one other American in Great Britain that night. Muhammad Ali was scheduled to fight Henry Cooper at Wembley Stadium. Marshall was able to get seven tickets for a closed circuit showing in a movie theatre not far from our hotel. I can tell you that Ali won the fight. I can't tell you exactly what round. What I do remember is much more vivid. Don, Lew, Phil, and I, along with the Tennessee Three, Marshall,

Luther Perkins, and W.S. Holland were the seven that used the tickets. When "God Save the Queen" was played before the match, the entire audience rose to its feet. That is all but seven. When the "Star-Spangled Banner" was played, we seven lone Americans stood up in that crowded hall. You have to remember this was the Viet Nam war era and Americans were viewed with a jaundiced eye. We could feel it. To this day it's hard to explain the feeling. It was a little fear, a little caution, and a little pride. Looking back we knew we'd done the right thing by standing up for America.

As I said before, the memory doesn't always have to be big. We were traveling late one night somewhere in the wilds of Wisconsin heading toward Chicago. We would take turns driving while the other three would try to sleep a little till their turn came. It was Don's turn. Now my brother has never aspired to be a NASCAR driver nor cared too much about driving in general. He did then and still does use it as a necessary means of going from one place to the other. To him, it's no more or less important than that. We three were pretty soon sound asleep. That didn't last long. We were jolted awake when the car began shaking like we were traveling on a dirt road. You know what? We were on a dirt road. In the Chicago area there are interstates, interchanges, loops and cloverleaves, but my brother found a dirt road. Phil was the first to react by asking, "Where in the hell are we, D.S.?" (He's always called Don by his initials.)

Now Phil, ever-aware of the geography around him determined where we were and how to get back on the right route. Don, who laughed about it that night and still laughs about it to this day, was unfazed. Quite simply he'd rather be writing a song.

★ ★ ★ ★

I wouldn't be honest if I weren't able to disclose some of my own shortcomings, certainly not all, but some. We had only been with the Cash show less than a year when I was faced with a situation that was a little uncomfortable. We were playing Greenville, North Carolina. Greenville, not being a major market, was not attended by John's manager, Saul Holiff. Marshall Grant would ordinarily settle the box office in his absence but Marshall was also away on a rare family emergency. John asked if I would meet with the promoter and take care of the settlement.

Now comes one of my many deficiencies: I'm not good at even basic math. It has never been easy for me. You can tell me what year I was born and I can't even tell you how old I am. Anyway, I, of course, told John I'd be glad to help out and then went to Phil (who is so good with figures that we nicknamed him "Mr. Numbers") and asked him to literally back me up. I arrived at the box office, went in like I knew exactly what I was doing and Phil went along but stood behind the promoter. The gentleman ran down a list of deductions, taxes and expenses and all of them in percentage form. If he would say 16 and a half percent, I'd look across his shoulder and Phil would either shake his head yes or no. The guy never knew the difference. It wasn't the last time we did that through the years. It works. If you don't believe me, get Phil and try it sometime.

★ ★ ★ ★

There is no one who admires the talents of all four of my Brothers more than me. I was always the least musical of all of us and every one of them has helped me before when I was musically challenged. It simply didn't come as quickly or as naturally for me as it did for them. I remember once when we were doing impressions in our show, Lew asked, "Harold, do you realize you sing better when you're doing Ernie Ford?" I said, "Well, I reckon. He's a better singer than I am."

★ ★ ★ ★

I should mention that a lot of the true pleasure in our business comes from meeting and getting to know people you wouldn't otherwise come in contact with. We've always been movie fans so it was a special treat for us to be playing the Hollywood Bowl in the late 60s. And there were more thrills to come. Don, Lew and I were standing out back after our portion of the show, when we looked up and saw Jack Palance and Lee Marvin walk up to us and proceed to tell us how much they enjoyed the performance. Lee Marvin went on to name obscure, early singles of ours that he owned. Friends, it *don't* get much better than that. I ran up the steps to the dressing room to tell Phil that two major movie stars were downstairs and see if he wanted to meet them. He said, "Yeah, I'll probably be down there after while." He never came down. We still kid him about it, but like I told you before, he ain't easy to explain.

★ ★ ★ ★

No one from the outside world would ever suspect that Phil and Carl Perkins almost reached comedy team status in private. Through mutual respect they kept us laughing on buses, backstage and in hotel rooms. Phil called him Uncle Carl while Carl referred to Phil as "you little idiot." With reference to Andy Clyde from the Hopalong Cassidy movies, Carl would tell Phil, "When you get old you're gonna look just like California." If we would happen to be in a hotel room, Phil would stand up, take off his pants and grab Carl's toupee. He'd place it on his knee and talk to it. I can't tell you what Carl would say to that but it was hilarious.

Carl was a handsome man without the hairpiece but we could never convince him of that. As soon as Phil would spot Carl anywhere, he'd run over to him, lean down and stare up at his forehead. Carl would back up self-consciously and say, "You're lookin' up under that thing, aren't you?" We would all laugh but I got the distinct feeling that we were exceptions. I don't think everyone in the world could have gotten away with that.

We took turns entertaining each other both on and off the stage. It helped us pass the time when we were so far away from home. It also made some lifetime friends.

★ ★ ★ ★

We were having fun seeing the world, exploring America and working on our career. It wasn't always easy, but we watched our pennies and somehow made it work. I had three girls at the time, Kim, Karmen, and Kodi, and brought home all I could. For years I had represented a custom-tailored clothing line out of Chicago. I designed all the Statler suits; I outfitted the Tennessee Three, Carl Perkins, and, of course, Johnny Cash. So when John started his ABC network show, I designed the first long, black frock coat he ever had. I had it tailored and fitted. He was very pleased and proud and it became a trademark with him. It's a little piece of country music trivia. I created all our fancy suits and had them tailored through the 70s and early 80s.

Looking back through these memories pulls at the heart strings. We loved what we did, but loved going home at the end of a tour. You see, that's what kept our heart strings in tune. We could always go back to Virginia. After a week or two we were recharged and refreshed and could go back to what we'd prayed for all our young lives. Home. It was the way we kept our perspective and our sanity.

It's a unique place to grow up. People in the Old Dominion state and more specifically in our Shenandoah Valley, have a great sense of being. We are not snobbish or prejudiced, but very aware of where things take place. It's summed up in one of my favorite stories about my dad. He and I had listened to and admired the Chuck Wagon Gang for years. We would get up early in the mornings and listen to pre-dawn broadcasts. Gospel music was scarce, so you had to make a point to find it. Finally, several years go by and the Chuck Wagon Gang is scheduled to sing in Harrisonburg, Virginia, in person. I was excited and went to Dad with the news. He said he probably wouldn't go. I said, "But Dad, you've always said if they were ever anywhere close you were going to see them and it's only 25 miles to Harrisonburg." He said, "I know son, but they just ain't close enough." Like I said, it matters to us where you are.

For instance, if you ask someone about an old school friend and you inquire, "How is Tom doing?" they answer, "Tom is working in Washington and married a girl from South Carolina." They tell you this before answering that Tom is doing just fine. I'm reminded of a wonderful friend, Jack Young, who went on to heaven several years ago to question and inspire the angels. He worked for a company at home that wanted to promote him to a position in New York City. He asked the corporate head, "Isn't everyone in New York trying to save their money so they can retire to a home in the mountains of Virginia?" The reply was, "Yes, probably." Jack said, "I'll stay here. I've already got a home in Virginia." Think about it. It makes sense to us.

There's a small blessing that hangs on many parlor walls here that reads: *To be a Virginian either by birth, marriage, adoption or even on one's mother's side, is an introduction to any state in the union, a passport to any foreign country and a benediction from above.*

Roots. You can travel, explore and overstay your welcome but you're always pulled back where you belong. Some people say one place is as good as another. We say you're always better off being at home.

Chapter Seven

The Class of '57 had its dreams
But livin' life day to day is never like it seems
Things get complicated when you get past eighteen
But the Class of '57 had its dreams
— Harold Reid and Don Reid
"Class of '57"

— Don —

June 18, 1965, one year, three months and ten days after our debut night in the big leagues with the Johnny Cash Show in Canton, Ohio, we were in Carnegie Hall at the New York Folk Festival. "Flowers on The Wall" started to hit a few months later and we were thrown simultaneously to the top of the pop and country charts. We were touring and recording and doing all the West Coast and East Coast TV music shows while being sought to do national TV and radio commercials and we were trying to do it all.

"Who put eight great tomatoes in that little bitty can? - Contadina®." Remember that tomato paste commercial on TV in the sixties? That was we. Or how about:

"Them other guys got seven sticks but Beech-nut® gives you eight.
Eight sticks for the price of seven, (ain't) ain't that great?"

That was the 'yours truly' group also, but this time selling chewing gum. And there were more. We did McDonald's® jingles and Dr. Pepper® commercials. The ones we always turned down were the beer ads. None of us drank and we were very adamant about any sponsorship that related to alcohol. Years later in the 70s and 80s when it became popular to have your tours sponsored and paid for by big corporations, we turned down big money offers from beer companies and sponsored our own. Even later in the 90s when we did a television series, we had a clause in our contract that prohibited beer ads from running during our hour on the air each week.

Even with all that we were doing, the Grammy® nominations took us by surprise. We got four nominations, two in the country field and two in the pop field and were asked to perform at the awards show in Nashville. And that night in March of 1966 when we flew out of Toronto in the middle of a tour to Nashville for the big event, these four Shenandoah Valley boys knew very little of what to expect. We had our fingers crossed for the country categories—Best Country Single and Best New Country Artist—but the two in the pop field were Best Performance by a Vocal Group and Best Contemporary Performance by a Group and we were pitted against the likes of The Beatles, Herman's Hermits, The Supremes, and Sam the Sham and the Pharaohs. It was our first star-studded award show and we sort of melted into the crowd and became watchers until they called us up to sing and then started calling out the winners. We took home two out of four that night. One for Best New Country Artist and one of the pop awards against those people we thought we had no chance of beating. We stayed up practically all night, not partying, but just talking to each other about what was happening to us, then got up and did all the morning interview shows and flew back to Canada and finished the tour.

Our direction was the next question to address. We had offers coming from every big agency in the country; from all the Vegas showrooms; from TV shows for more guest appearances; and from people who wanted to promote our own tours for us. We had every door open to us but we had a debt to repay. For the first time we were now a marquee asset and we had a chance to pay John back for believing in us when nobody else cared. So we stayed with the Cash show.

We also did outside things from time to time when it appealed to us. We sang a couple of songs in a little movie called *That Tennessee Beat*. (If you haven't seen it, don't look for it. Each time it's played it does more harm to the ozone layer.) We played major fair dates by ourselves in the summer months. (This is where we developed a friendship with Ernie Ford. We performed, then he came out and then he'd call us back and we'd do a few numbers together. What was always entertaining to me was that old slow-talkin' Ern from East Tennessee onstage, became Mr. Hollywood offstage. It went from "you little pea-picker" to "Hey, baby" in a culture shocking flash.)

We flew out to the West Coast to do the *Joey Bishop Show*, which had taken on Johnny Carson in the late nighttime slot on ABC. We were booked for a Friday night with plans of coming home that weekend. But after our one song, Joey asked on camera what we were doing all next week. Harold said, "We've got a luncheon date in Omaha Tuesday, why what you got in mind?" and got a big laugh at Joey's expense. But he loved it and invited us to perform on every show the next week. The only problem was we each had one suit with us and we were wearing them at the time. This was more of a problem then because at the time we were dressing alike, so we couldn't just go out and shop for clothes. We had closets full of stage clothes back in Virginia 3,000 miles away. That night, before the show ever even aired on the east coast, we got on the phone and had each of our wives box up five suits, shirts, ties, pairs of boots, and all the everyday clothes we would need for a week, and air mail them to us at our hotel. We probably spent more in air freight than we made off the Bishop Show but we had a great time that week with other guests like Lee Marvin and John Houston and Muhammad Ali and, of course, Regis Philbin, who was Joey's Ed McMahon. (A couple of notes you might find interesting: Lee Marvin always carried cigarettes in his sock. Don't ask me. And every time we ran into Ali, be it a TV show or a restaurant or an airplane, he wanted to spar with Harold. And then he'd always put his arm around him and say the same thing. He'd say, "Now I don't want you to take offense to this, but you look just like the bass singer for the Temptations." And Harold would invariably say, "I don't take offense to that at all but just what do you think I'm going to do about it if I did, Champ?")

★ ★ ★ ★

All through the mid to late 60s, although we were working a lot and staying busy on the road, our recording career was suffering. Harold and Lew and I were writing like madmen but we couldn't seem to follow the big hit. One reason was that Columbia Records kept giving us different producers and no one would let us record our own material. We charted in the top ten a number of times during our subsequent years there, but not with what you would consider a bona fide hit.

We were still doing all of John's record sessions with him, which took us to Folsom Prison for the big one and then to San Quentin for the follow-up. From prison we would then go do Billy Graham Crusades and then a White House performance for President Nixon. So life was never dull even though we were feeling the pressures and struggles of the recording industry.

Billy Graham was all you wanted him to be; as good a man away from the pulpit as he was behind it. Once we were finishing up a three week tour of one-nighters and the final night was his Crusade in Dallas. We were tired and anxious to get home and had booked the latest flight possible out of Love Field at 10 p.m. That afternoon at the run-through we told Billy our situation; that if we stayed for the whole service we would miss our plane and couldn't get another flight till noon the next day. He said, "Boys, after you sing, you just cut out of here," and graciously let us off the hook. Understand, we wanted to stay for the sermon, but we wanted to head that jet east for Virginia pretty badly, too.

President Nixon, on the other hand, showed little emotion during the entire East Room concert yet was very friendly afterward and even honored the four of us later with an official invitation to San Clemente.

Somewhere along in here, about late 1968, John came to us and said he was cleaning up his act. It was sort of like a confession. He said he was putting his demons behind him and was going to become the biggest thing in the business. He thanked us for sticking with him during some rough years but promised us we'd never see the old Johnny again. We never did.

The next summer, ABC hired *The Johnny Cash Show* as the seasonal replacement show for the *Glen Campbell Goodtime Hour*. Then it got picked up as a regular series the next January for two years. All of this good news had its shrouded moments. We were living in Virginia and the TV show was taped 500 miles away in Nashville, which had already become a second home to us but not like it would in the near future. We all had young children and absolutely no desire to relocate, so our weekly schedule became: rehearse Monday through Wednesday, tape Thursday nights at the Ryman Auditorium, leave at midnight after the show and drive back to Staunton, have most of the weekend there, leave Sunday afternoon and drive back to Nashville for rehearsals. This cycle was never broken except when John wanted to work a Friday and Saturday night and then we weren't home for weeks at a time.

The steady flow of guest stars the show brought into Nashville each week was entertainment unto itself. The old established acts such as Bob Hope and Louis Armstrong and Peggy Lee to the young up-and-comers like Liza Minnelli, Linda Ronstadt and The Monkees. Each week was an adventure in human behavior.

Random memories

• Dale Robertson, taking time off from his Western movies and TV shows, decided he wanted to sing. So he came on and sang Glen's "Gentle On My Mind." This was fine until he saw us there and decided he wanted us to sing it with him. This was fine, too, until he insisted we sing the phrasing to his liking which was the exact faltering clip with which he talked. Therefore the song came out sounding like a record with a skipping needle.

• Neil Diamond, a nice Jewish boy who wrote some terrific songs and had some great hits, walked into a variety show format he wasn't expecting. We were all supposed to line up at the end and sing an old gospel song which happened to be Albert E. Brumley's "I'll Fly Away." Neil wound up standing between us and to our surprise had never heard this song that the rest of the Southern cast had cut their musical teeth on. We gave him a quick course in the lyric and he faked it through, and was very good, I might add; better than we would have been with "Hava Nagila."

• It had become my job to introduce all the acts to the studio audience and serve as emcee as I always did on the road shows. The Statlers would do the warm-up before each taping began and keep the in-house crowd from getting restless. Ray Charles was in the wings and I told him I would introduce him and then he would be pre-set for the cameras and then John would introduce him again for the TV audience. So I simply said, "Ladies and Gentlemen, the incomparable Ray Charles," and he was led to his piano stool to thunderous applause. But when it died down he turned to his assistant and said in the mike, "What dat dat man call me?"

• George Gobel, whom I had laughed at as a kid with his 'spooky ole Alice' routines every Saturday night, was a great source of entertainment for the four of us backstage as well as on stage. He would shuffle slowly from the dressing room to the wings with a glass of whatever in his hand, barely lifting or even moving his feet, and stand and wait for his cue. When his introduction came, he would ditch the glass and bounce out on the stage as alert and lively as a puppy at mealtime. Then on his exit, that energy would wane as soon as he cleared the curtain. The glass would appear magically back in his hand and he'd shuffle back to the dressing room completely oblivious to anything else around him. But what a funny man.

• During this time, the whole cast went out to Old Tucson, Arizona, the old Western town Columbia Pictures built as a movie set back in 1939 which has served for some of the better Western films ever made. We spent a week there

with some great stars associated with the genre: Walter Brennan, Andy Devine, Kirk Douglas, Roy Rogers and Dale Evans. Kirk Douglas did a scene with Harold as the bartender and encouraged him to do more acting. And he was pretty good the best I remember. Kirk also showed us some great gun twirling tricks: the twirl, then over the shoulder, the twirl and then into the holster and never looking. I practiced this move for the next six months in my living room, in hotel rooms, in any spare time I could find and believe it or not got pretty good at it. Not better than Kirk, but then I wouldn't want to.
• Jack Palance did the show. What he did I can't for the life of me remember, but what I do remember was that he stalked around backstage and scared the makeup girls and hairdressers so badly that one of us had to sit in the room with them anytime he was being made up or having his hair combed. I think he just enjoyed seeing how far he could carry his stage persona into real life.
• I came out of my hotel room one day and found Stevie Wonder and his band in the hall playing tag with all of them hollering, "Stevie's it! Stevie's it!"
• But the saddest was one morning at breakfast in the hotel dining room where we'd all eat together. We were sitting at the table next to Louis Armstrong who had turned the ole Ryman into Preservation Hall the night before. He was aged and in his last year of life and appeared tired and weakened but he was still Satchmo to all of us. A fan was making the rounds of the tables and we were all signing her little book when she took it to his table and said, "May I have your autograph?" He said, "Sure, honey," and proceeded to give her his address. She corrected him and said, "No sir. Not your address. Your autograph." I wanted to get up and go over and hug him but instead I just sat there and looked the other way. After all he was the King of Jazz.

Chapter Eight

But he's in country music where he always wanted to be
— Harold Reid and Don Reid
"Where He Always Wanted To Be"

— Harold —

As Don mentioned to you a little earlier, we were busy. We were touring with John, doing dates on our own, and were still able to write and record God-given hit records. As I think back, it looks hectic, but when you're living it, you're just glad to be able to do what you love. We were still with the Columbia label and when "Flowers" made the big crossover, it gave us a warped view of our first million seller. I say warped because it seemed to us that we should do that crossover thing every time. It *ain't* that easy.

You could tell this by the releases that followed: "My Darlin' Hildegard," "The Right One," "Half A Man." Now don't run out and try to buy these. I don't say this because I don't want your business; I tell you this because I don't want you to listen to them too closely. Musically, they were fine, but you could hear us struggling to top what had set our standard. It all goes back to the question that everyone asks themselves after their first big record, "Should it sound like or should it sound different?" By the way, no one to this day has that answer.

At Columbia we were shuffled between studios, producers, song suggestions and general disinterest. (The latter is what record companies are best at.) We had a five-year deal that was running out fast, but not too fast for us. We put our heads together and decided to go label shopping. Now when you've been around for a few years and spent some long hours in a recording studio, you become acquainted with a lot of great musicians. In fact, they are the best of the best. There was a brilliant guitar player who'd boosted our instrumental tracks with his unusual upright dobro. He was a nice guy, a producer and a vice-president across the street at Mercury Records. It was a place to start. Enter Jerry Kennedy.

I picked up the phone one day, called Jerry and told him we had to get away from Columbia and asked if he was interested. He never hesitated. He said, "Yes, but I'm so busy that you guys would have to come up with your own material." Now I don't know how much you folks know about singers, writers and recording artists, but for Jerry to give us that alternative is like telling the fox there's a padlock on the gate but you've left the back door to the hen house wide open. We jumped in with all eight feet.

I well remember the evening in Nashville we Brothers went to a restaurant and discussed with great care and resolution how we would handle this new opportunity. I can sum it up in one sentence. We were going to be strictly country. No more pop or crossover targets, just country like we'd always wanted to be.

I had been carrying around a country song I'd written about two years before and we decided it would be our new single and our new statement. So in 1970 we recorded our first song, "Bed Of Rose's," for our new label and crossed our fingers. Now don't get ahead of me here, but I'm sure you've already guessed it. "Bed Of Rose's" was one of the biggest selling country records that year and it immediately crossed over and wound up on the pop charts, too. You can't plan these things. It's another thing in our business no one knows the answer to.

★ ★ ★ ★

It was during this period of time in our career that we encountered that small black cloud that would grow as time moved on—Lew's health. He had

60

complained a long time about his stomach and the pain he suffered, so when it became unbearable for him one night in Omaha, we were forced to finish the tour and leave him there in the hospital. They kept him a week and we made arrangements to have him flown home. The diagnosis was severe ulcers. He was okay for a while, but it came back again and again.

Lew was an only child of Lewis, Sr. and Rose DeWitt. They both had their share of health problems, but never ulcers. So we kept moving on although Lew wasn't always up to the task. We three—Don, Phil, and I—tried to take up the slack and do all we could to keep it together for him, for us, and for the fans.

★ ★ ★ ★

We went back to Europe in '72 and learned a little more how the other half lives. We had had fish and chips in London (wrapped in newspaper—delicious!), but when we arrived in Oslo, Norway, one morning, our hotel restaurant announced their catch-of-the-day was whale steak. My brother, Don, ever the adventurer, had one for breakfast. I won't go into detail, but I can tell you that before dinner that poor dead whale was able to surface one last time.

Whenever you fly across several time zones, it does something to your body and your mind. It's called jet lag and we had a pretty good case of it that spring when we arrived. We were writing an idea for a new album titled *Country Music: Then and Now.* It was to be just what it sounded like—a look back. We began talking about the very early Saturday morning radio shows that featured local and not-very-good talent. We wrote and laughed and finally went to bed declaring we'd get up the next morning and read what we'd written and if it was still funny, we'd use it. It was. So when we flew home after that tour, there were five of us. Harold, Phil, Lew, Don and Lester 'Roadhog' Moran. He would take on a life of his own.

The album was recorded with about ten minutes devoted to the Roadhog. It was an instant success. Everyone loved Lester's brash attitude and his band, The Cadillac Cowboys. I did the gruff voice of Hog while Don was Wesley, Phil was Red, and Lew was Wichita. We gave each of them a personality and they gave Country Music another group. Here is a reprint of actual bios that we created and sent out with publicity for the record.

Lester 'Roadhog' Moran

Lester Moran was born 49 $^1/_2$ years ago in a farm house in the United States. When Lester was only 23 years old his father left home along with his mother. Lester was taken in by a wino uncle who taught Lester all he knew about the fiddle. To this day Lester has never had a lesson or learned one. When Lester was only 33, his uncle left home along with his aunt and Lester knew this could only mean one thing—he was being called into Country Music.

Lester's hobbies are watching wrestling and roller derby on TV and sucker fishing. He lists his favorite food as sardines and crackers and mashed potatoes with gravy. His favorite color is green and his favorite singer, of course, Lee Moore, of course. Lester is married to the formal Ruby Lee Armstrong whom he met while they were in service. They have one child, Ethel Renee. They reside in a semi-modest, prefab cottage bungalow just outside of Rainbow Valley close to Lester's work. Lester's greatest ambition in life is to meet and shake hands with Doug Kershaw because as Lester says, "It takes one to know one."

Raymond 'Wichita' Ramsey

Wichita grew up in a musical family. His fondest memories are of playing in the family band at church socials, parties and square dances. Wichita boasts that his father played four instruments: upright bass, electric bass, electric guitar, and flattop guitar. His mother played accordion and his sister played around.

When his family retired from the business due to public demand, Wichita joined up with Lester and formed one of the most sought after duets in the history of Rainbow Valley. Wichita, the original member of the Cadillac Cowboys, passes his many leisure hours playing pinball machines and Kilroy pool. His favorite color is black because of his favorite actor, Lash LaRue. His favorite food is hot dogs with mustard and plenty of onions. Wichita's greatest ambition is to learn to play all the chords in "Whispering." Wichita lives at home with his mother and enjoys wearing Western clothes. Wichita's favorite all-around entertainer is Buck Owens of whom Wichita says, "Nobody writes a song like ole Buck."

Henry 'Red' Vines

Henry 'Red' Vines is the ladies man of the group. He was born 37 years ago to foster parents and spent his early years learning the music trade. He plays rhythm guitar and a little banjo. Red has played with humorous bands. Among some of the more famous ones, Biff Bradley and the All-Star Wildcats, Ramblin' Ray and the Ranch House Boys, and Woody Burns and the Gospel Flames. Woody once said of Red, "If Red was the last guitar player on earth, I'd hire him."

Red is not married and has two children, Teddy and Doyle Vines. Pitching horseshoes and do-it-yourself projects are Red's hobbies. His favorite color is white and his favorite pastime is listening to records. His favorite singer is the Wilburn Brothers. Red's greatest ambition is to buy a new car.

Wesley W. Rexrode

Wesley was born to normal parents when he was very young. Wesley was educated at the Union State Detention Home for Boys and received two full years and one black Sunday of high school at the Frank Mull Reformatory for Men. (He also received two years once for women.) Wesley learned his musical prowess from a 'roommate' during one of those lengthy stays.

Wesley is married to the formal Queenie Ramsey, sister of Wichita, who was Wesley's connection to his current position as a Cadillac Cowboy. Wesley has often said of Queenie, "If it hadn't been for Queenie, I wonder where I'd be today."

Wesley's pet peeve is unmarked police cars. His favorite color is chrome. His favorite singer is Robert Mitchum. His favorite food and comedian is Jimmy Dean and sausage. His favorite song is "The Girl Who Invented Kissing," the old Hank Snow classic. His hobbies include making billfolds and license plates. Wesley and Queenie reside in a temporary residence in Rainbow Valley. When asked his one ambition in life, Wesley confided he'd always wanted one of those 19" color TVs.

Clubs began to spring up that required all their members to speak like the Hog, "Mighty fine, mighty fine." Even with all this attention, we were still surprised when a Mercury VP flew to Nashville from Chicago to take us to dinner one night. His mission? The label wanted Lester and his boys to record their own album. Look out world here comes the Hog!

To include Lester on an album for ten minutes is fun, but for Lester to stand on his own very unsteady feet for roughly an hour, takes some thought. So we had to come up with something besides the off-key music. One of the segments is an open musical letter to Jerry Kennedy as the Hog promotes some local talent. It's officially called "Rainbow Valley Confidential Audition Tape." And it features every stereotype known to man.

For this we set an ancient, reel-to-reel tape recorder on the floor and let it run uninterrupted from start to finish just like we imagined Lester would do. It featured the duo of Briscoe and Snuffy Lamont (Lew and Phil), who are neither trained nor housebroken but would sound very uptown to the Hog. Then there's Mrs. Viola Wheeler (Lew), who sings opera but only in her mind. The poetry is by Willard Wiseman (Don), who can't read fast enough to keep up with his stylish image. We all grabbed an instrument to portray Dexter Dull and The Sharp Tones and I think you'll agree there's nothing sharp about them.

All this was done in Don's recently remodeled 1877 Queen Anne home. Did I mention the floor where the tape recorder sat was a hardwood floor that was as beautiful as the rest of the house? Well, it was. The last audition the Hog introduces is Cletis Duncan, a tap dancer. I played Cletis and all I know about tap dancing is what I've watched Donald O'Connor do in the movies. My only preparation was that I'd worn shoes with taps so I started clogging on Don's hardwood floor. Now my brother is down on his knees motioning for me to keep going till we run out of tape. I don't know how long it actually was, but it seemed like hours to me.

When we finished, there was a three foot square area on this beautiful floor that looked like it had been beaten with that log chain John used on his table. I felt bad, but Don said, "Don't worry. I wouldn't have it any other way." He must have meant it. The house was sold ten years later and the dents and scratches were still there.

Lester 'Roadhog' Moran and the Cadillac Cowboys would never have been complete if we hadn't included a live concert. So we did. We decided that the local dance at the Johnny Mack Brown High School would be perfect. We included music, dancing and a fight. Like everything else, we did it only once. For about two weeks we collected all of our soft drink bottles on the bus and took them with us to record Lester's live dance. All the secretaries in the building at Mercury helped out. They were in the studio for background noise and voices. We set up two four-by-eight panels of wallboard as a barrier and when the fight broke out, we all threw our saved-up bottles against the wall. The sound effects were great but there was a half-inch of broken glass on the floor. It was effective, it was dangerous, and it was a mess. The regular custodian refused to clean it up, so we had to hire outside help. But boy, it was fun.

Even our record company caught the spirit of what we were doing. You may or may not know that a Gold Album is awarded to an artist for sales in excess of 500,000 and a Platinum Album is awarded for sales in excess of 1,000,000. In April of '81 Mercury presented Lester and his gang with a Plywood Album for sales of 1250. My sense of humor tells me to leave it right there. My ego tells me I should inform you that it was a very successful project, closer to Gold than Plywood, but it made the Hog happy just the same. Like I said about this business, don't try to understand it, just enjoy it.

★ ★ ★ ★

It was the same year our world travels would allow us to spend the night in Naples, Italy, and then sit on Waikiki Beach in Hawaii. We visited New Zealand and Australia while we racked up our air mileage points. You can only cover that kind of territory on an airplane and sometimes it's not all that pleasant. Like the night we left California after recording the San Quentin album with J.R. We raced to the airport to catch a late night cross-country flight to Dulles International in Washington, D.C. It started about fifteen minutes after we took off. The pilot came on to say it might be a little bumpy. That wasn't just an understatement; it was an outright lie. The plane and all its victims literally tossed and turned for the next four-and-a-half hours. Everyone was a little uptight. I was scared to death. We had had some bad experiences before (once my Brothers had physically restrained me from going into the cockpit after a pilot), but this flight was the worst. About forty minutes out of Washington, the plane took a sharp dive to the right, upsetting a table of hot coffee in the aisle. The flight attendant screamed and fell onto a passenger. I said a prayer and resigned myself to the fact that I would never pick up my car in the airport lot because dead men don't drive. But through some miracle we finally landed and everyone agreed it was as bad as it gets. It had its worst effect on me so it was no surprise a few months later when we would leave the Cash show, our first purchase would be a bus. All my Brothers said if we couldn't make it by bus, we just wouldn't do it. They did that for me and me alone. I will forever be grateful to them for that. It was a magnanimous thing for them to do. It made me work even harder. We really were 'brothers.'

Chapter Nine

You can't go home to the good times
You can't go home anymore
Everything has changed, and who is there to blame
For the fact that you just can't go home
— Don Reid
"You Can't Go Home"

— Don —

Even if you never leave home, you still can't go back to the way it was. To those tender young memories and sweet summer evenings and the people and places you grew up cherishing. But we came as close as humanly possible. By never leaving our hometown we stayed surrounded with the old friends and the familiar landmarks and the family closeness that we had always known. Harold and I are two of three children. We have a sister, Faye Hemp, who also still lives right here in town. Our parents, Sidney and Frances, were hard-working people and Mom always saw that the three of us were in church every Sunday morning and in school every Monday morning and gave us what, looking back on, seems to be a picture-perfect, 1950s childhood right out of a nostalgic TV sit-com. I'm sure it wasn't that much of a snap for them, but then we all tend to get lost in the good memories and put the bad ones to bed early.

Our dad had an affectionate habit of nicknaming the people he loved. He never called anyone by their given name even if he had been the one who had given it to them, such as us kids. But even before we came along, he called his brother 'Gov'ner,' his sister 'Kitty,' and our Mother 'Maggie,' which had no remote connection to her name at all. So in the ensuing years of our childhood, my sister and brother and I learned to answer to whatever he decided to call us. Faye was 'Jitterbug,' Harold was 'Buck,' and I was 'Pete.' (I thought that might clear up a couple of questions you've had since the beginning of the book.)

Daddy died in the summer of '67, right in the reflective heat of our first burst of success. He enjoyed what he saw but he would have loved what was going to happen to us. Many times in subsequent years in the frenzy of an awards show or the quietness of the bus lounge in the a.m. hours rolling down the highway in the middle of the desert, Harold and I would look at one another and say, "What I wouldn't give for Daddy to see this." Mom, on the other hand, was with us through it all but was as unaffected by it all as anyone could possibly be. She was the opposite of a stage mother. She never offered to anyone that she was our mom; never made a big deal over the people we were able to introduce her to; and always kept us firm and balanced about anything that may be happening in our world. She was the most loving and sweetest person ever to touch our lives and she lived to the wonderful and healthy age of 92 and saw all three of her children retire. Not many parents are allowed to do that. We lost her in the spring of 2004 and that's what I mean by not being able to go home even though we never left.

★ ★ ★ ★

I was riding around the park in Staunton with my wife, Gloria, and our year-old son, Debo, on July Fourth in 1969 and was surprised to see how quiet it was. Except for a few scattered picnickers, it was like any other lazy summer afternoon. I told my Brothers about this a few days later and we began to visualize that this situation might be the answer to one of our fastest-growing problems. Since we had begun to have some national success and were staying busy with regular and extensive tours, we found that all the local requests that we used to be able to fulfill were now practically impossible to see to. Charities, clubs, churches, fund-raisings of any kind always called us to come by and sing a few songs and draw some people and attention to their cause. We had begun to wean ourselves from many of them as we just no longer had the time and we also knew that if we continued to honor every call, pretty soon our appearance would mean nothing to anyone. So with our heads together we came up with an idea of one big show to take care of all the charities that wanted to get involved. We would perform, they would set up their booths to sell food and crafts and at the end of the day everyone would be happy. But where to start.

Harold took the idea to our old friend, Ray Houser, a local entertainer and community pillar and Ray said, "Funny you should bring that up. The mayor and I have been talking about setting aside a day to honor the Statlers." So that same week, Harold, Phil, Ray, and I met with Mayor Richard Farrier and the groundwork for our annual Happy Birthday USA celebration that would last for the next 25 years was laid. Never again could you ride around our little town on the Fourth of July and marvel at how quiet it was and wonder where all the people were. They were here!

That first year was like giving birth. We paced and worried about the crowd. We paced and worried about the weather as the event was outside in the city football stadium. We had put together a top-notch committee of some prominent and hard-working citizens and we weren't concerned about them doing their jobs. It was the crowd we felt most responsible for. Even Jesus noted that a prophet is without honor in his hometown.

We weren't prophets but we were feeling what he meant. We were beginning to draw crowds all over the country and we didn't want someone dropping the ball and cause us to be embarrassed at home. And we weren't. That first year there was a nice respectable crowd of Stauntonians to the tune of about 2500. We were satisfied. But they wanted more. How about a commitment to make this an annual event? The pressure was on but we said yes without really knowing what lay ahead.

We always kept a strict touring policy of never repeating a town for at least a year or eighteen months. This kept you fresh and kept you from wearing a hole in the municipal welcome mat. Also, after playing one area or city two or three times, we liked to give it a rest for a year or two before we went back. We had adopted this strategy after seeing so many of our fellow entertainers burn themselves out in areas that once were good for them but became ho-hum after they played them to death every three or four months. And now we were promising to perform every year for only God knows how long in the most important town in our lives. We would sing there only one night a year but live there all year long. So we had to be good. We had to be better each year or this thing would blow up in our collective face.

Well, it blew up but it was all in a good way. Each year the crowds grew until we were having 100,000 people for the concert. They would come days in advance and camp out. They would come from all over the world. They would quadruple Staunton's population for a three-day period, we would wave the flag and sing and everyone went away a little happier than they came. We began asking guests to appear with us and the trick here was it was all for charity. When the guests came they came at their own expense. We provided hotel rooms and that was it. But what most of the public never knew was that we would trade out dates with all of our guests. That was the deal we made. You do our charity event and then we'll do yours any place in the U.S. No money was ever exchanged, only favors. And we had some great guests—Reba, Tammy Wynette, Conway Twitty, Jerry Reed, and Barbara Mandrell. It got to be such an event that people would ask us if they could come sing. And one of the first ones to do that was Johnny Cash.

Rain was our biggest enemy. Each year we were sure we would raise thousands of dollars for the local charities, but the weather was something we could never relax about. After three years we moved the event to the baseball field to accommodate the growing attendance. And it was always a major decision whether we would open the show or have our guests open. It was our show and closing was the natural thing to do but then it might look as if we were giving the star spot to ourselves and not our guests. So one year we decided we would open and let our special guest close the show. That was the year Charley Pride had flown in on his private plane with his band and was raring to go. We went out and performed our portion and after our last song I introduced Charley. He came out and sang one song, "Kiss An Angel Good Morning" best I remember, and the heavens opened up and flooded everything that wasn't a duck in minutes. One song. So the next year we went back to getting our guests on early.

The Fourth of July became a national event in our hometown. The TV networks came to town to cover it. We did a live TV special around it with Crook and Chase. And every year it got bigger and more exciting and more stressful. Each year we would look at one another and say, "How long are we going to do this?" And we had no idea. Finally after twenty years we made a decision. We held a press conference and announced that we would do it for five more years, giving anyone a chance to attend who hadn't and giving those who had a few years left to savor the final events. So for a quarter of a century we played the same town every year. More years than not it rained, but the people, bless their hearts, always stayed and so did we.

— Harold —

As I look back over our career, I find there's a special place in my heart for our twenty-five years of hometown concerts on the Fourth. They were known all over the world as Happy Birthday U.S.A. What could be more special than being at home, having good friends and fellow entertainers come to visit, and have 100,000 local and out-of-town folks stop by to watch? And no money ever exchanged hands between the talent. Our guests would come free of charge. Then we would pay them back by playing their pet charity. No two were alike.

In 1975 we had Johnny Russell and Charlie McCoy as our guests. Russell's payback was that we recorded one of his songs. We recorded "You'll Be Back (Every Night In My Dreams)." It proved to be good for us both. It reached number three on the national charts. As for Charlie McCoy, we paid him back before he appeared with us on the night of July Fourth. We went to his hometown on July 2 and played a concert. It was a great day in a great community with a life-long friend. I say this with humility because when we left Fayetteville, West Virginia, the next morning, they had named their local ballpark Statler Field in our honor.

We had no better friend in our business than Conway Twitty. He appeared with us in Staunton in the summer of 1990. Sadly Conway died in 1993. It seemed even in death we were connected to our buddy. He passed away on June 5, Don's birthday. We paid back the appearance we owed a year later on August 21, my birthday. A reporter asked me once how I would sum up Conway. I told him that Conway was the kind of person who, as soon as your back was turned, would say something nice about you. I go on record as doing the same for him.

It's pretty well known that our little "Statler sister" was Barbara Mandrell. She knows how much we love her, so I can tell you the truth. She's pretty, talented and shrewd. Her daddy taught her well. I tell you this because I can prove it. Queenie, our pet nickname for her, appeared with us on July 4, 1979, and did a fantastic job as always. But when it came time for our payback, we were booked for her charity in Alabama for October 5, 6, and 7. We asked why *three* days and she said we were to play in a celebrity golf tournament two days after the concert. We told her that none of us played golf, which we truly didn't. She said not to worry about that, it would be fun so we stayed all three days. We met Gov. George Wallace and Presidential brother Billy Carter and it was our first encounter with actor

David Huddleston, a fellow Virginian, who guested on our TV show years later as the best Santa Claus ever. We became good friends. It was all worth the trip and very enjoyable but it didn't make us any better golfers. Well, maybe that's not true. Our teams consisted of four people: a pro, a celebrity, an amateur, and a contributor to the charity event. I told my team before we started that if they were very serious about this tournament, they'd better speak up now. They laughed and assured me it would be okay. We were playing best ball and without bragging, we did use one of my putts before coming in third for the whole thing. I received a beautiful leather golf bag and a gold-plated putter with my name on it. I've never played since but I don't understand why people make a big deal about golf. It seemed pretty easy to me.

— Don —

Staunton did a lot of nice things for us in commemoration of HBUSA. They built a monument with our likenesses in granite in the park; they built a permanent stage in the downtown area with four brass stools representing the ones we used on TV and in concert, and they named a street after us, Statler Boulevard. And the final year (1994), just before we went on stage for the last Fourth of July performance, I gave each Statler a ring I had had specially made for the occasion. They were made by the same folks who make the Super Bowl and World Series rings and look very much like them except ours have Statler logos and dates on the sides. Each of the four stones is a different color and thereafter we always wore them on stage. And as a final salute, I had the mold broken so there could never be another one made. So eBay®, forget about it. There are only four of them.

★ ★ ★ ★

1972 saw us winning our first Country Music Association Award (there would be eight more to come), our third Grammy®, and the beginning of a new era for the Statler career. The hit records were coming with a nice regularity, dates were pouring in and yet we were still fulfilling all of the Cash show tours. There was little time for anything but work and we realized something had to be done to give a little structure to our lives and our business. We talked to John, who was very aware of our situation and very understanding. He encouraged us to take whatever steps we needed to take and at the end of that year, we did. We left the Cash show and headed out on our own.

The first thing we did was buy a touring bus. We had flown for so many years and had so many bad experiences in the air that we just wanted to keep our feet on the ground for a while. We hired a driver, Dale Harman, whom we had known from high school, put together a band and in short time found an agent who would make one of the biggest differences in our business lives since that debut night in Canton, Ohio.

Major Dick Blake owned a booking agency in Nashville and was setting us on all the shows we wanted to work. But he shared a dream with us and that dream was to put together our own touring show, promote our own dates, and play the towns and buildings that we wanted to play. In other words we would send an advance man into a city to rent the auditorium or arena, buy the advertising and we then would control and own everything with no middle men to pay. Dick Blake handled all this on our behalf and became a close and loving friend. He had a unique mixture of a sense of humor and a sense of business. Every night when it was a sellout and not an empty seat to be found, he'd take off his hat and rub his head and say, "We're losing money tonight, Reverend." (He always called me Reverend because he said when I talked on stage I sounded like a preacher.) I'd say, "Losing money? It's standing room only." And he'd say, "Yeah, and that means we should have done a second show. No telling how many we turned away, so we're losing money." On our first tours, we had Tammy Wynette and Ronnie Milsap opening the shows. Then there was Barbara Mandrell, Brenda Lee, Reba McEntire. The best in the business were a part of our touring company through the years.

But Dick was in poor health due to World War II injuries. He had been a Japanese POW and had internal problems that left him physically frail, but with the heart of a giant. Travel was his biggest enemy and we tried to encourage him to stay in the office more and let us handle the road duties, but he was determined to do it all. However, help was on its way.

A short time before life took its final toll on Dick in the early 80s, a strange and unexpected thing happened to us. For the years, eight and half to be exact, that we were with the Johnny Cash show, Marshall Grant had been the bass player, road manager and straw boss of the entire troupe. Ever since we had left, which had been about ten years at the time, we had joked among ourselves that we wanted to find "a Marshall"—someone who would take charge and do all the things that needed to be done on a daily basis and be trusted with all the inner circle business and duties that arose. When through the grapevine we heard what we thought would never come to pass. John and Marshall, old and dear friends and business associates, had come to a parting of the ways. There had been hard feelings between the two, though we considered them both to be our friends, and now Marshall was at home in Mississippi with his feet propped up. We went by to see him and his wife, Etta, and he got on the bus and spent the weekend with us on tour. This happened a couple of times and everyone began to see a growing pattern here that might solve a lot of problems for the organization. If Marshall could travel with us, Dick could stay home more, book the tours and take better care of his health. And this is exactly what happened and how Marshall was there and in place when Dick passed away in '83. He picked up the mantle that Dick had left and we went into the next twenty years with "the Marshall" instead of a "facsimile Marshall."

Chapter Ten

How do you like your dream so far?
Is it all you thought it would be?
How do you like ridin' a star?
How do you like it so far?
— Harold Reid and Don Reid
"How Do You Like Your Dream So Far"

— Harold —

Life was good. We had already achieved the impossible once when we landed a place with the Cash organization. Now we had to do it again by stepping out into that deep water where no one ever swam before. At first we had been told that a group could never, ever be a feature act in country music. So it was beyond all expectations that the Statlers could possibly be headliners. We started to suspect it might be true as we ventured out into that deep unknown.

It was a very exciting time for us. We had left some dear friends in the Cash troupe but now met and worked with people who would also become good friends. Kitty Wells, Marty Robbins, Hank Thompson, Don Williams, Roy Acuff, Bobby Bare, Jerry Lee Lewis, Conway Twitty, Lynn Anderson, Carl Smith, Donna Fargo, Faron Young, Hank Snow and many, many more. Oh yes, and Gene Watson. (Excuse me George and Merle, but in my opinion Gene makes it a three-way tie.) All of them were wonderful people and most of them were great to work with.

We were also booked on large 'package' shows of the day. This was simply a promoter hiring two or more acts to present on a stage at the same time. The promoter would usually designate who would open, who would go on in the middle and who would close the show. We noticed that we were being asked more and more to close. That was not only a little pressure; it was a large compliment. But sometimes it backfired. I'll tell you this story that I've only told a few close friends over the years. The date was November 3, 1973. The town was Freeport, Illinois. We shared the bill that night with Ferlin Husky. Now let me explain something to you right here that you may or may not know. Ten years earlier, when we were completely unknown, we had performed one song on one of those package shows that featured Mel Tillis and Ray Price, both great entertainers, but also Ferlin Husky who closed the show that night and I mean closed it. He had it all—looks, talent, stage presence and a know-how that only comes from years of doing it. To say the least, Ferlin was a hero. We looked up to him and I personally was very upset when the promoter came to us before the show in Freeport and said Ferlin was to open and we were to close. Now don't get me wrong. I wasn't worried about following Ferlin, because quite honestly, we could follow anyone in our business. I was upset because I didn't think Ferlin should have to open for us. We might have been worthy but I didn't think we were *that* worthy. The rest of the story? Everything went great. Ferlin, being the gentleman and pro that he is, went out and did his regular fantastic job. We went out and did ours and the people loved it. I hugged Ferlin and told him how much I admired him. I'll never forget it. It was a bittersweet pill for me. There should be more people like Ferlin Husky in our business.

★ ★ ★ ★

We were in that period of our career where the word management continued to arise. I will go on record right now to tell you we always managed ourselves. We figured that four heads were better than one so we threw it out on the table and made our own decisions. The only rule was—we were always honest and worked hard to make sure the other guy didn't get hurt. Corny? Probably, but it was the way we operated.

We were booked once by an organization in Cherry Hill, New Jersey. It was a flat date. That means they were paying our going rate to come do a concert in their town. As it got closer to the date, we received an offer to guest on the Dean Martin TV show in Los Angeles. Remember I told you earlier that airplanes were out? Well, it's a long way from Jersey to California. So we called the people in Cherry Hill and told them our dilemma. They said we could postpone the date and we promised to make it up as soon as possible. We stayed in touch with them and it took about eighteen months to settle on a suitable time for the both of us. By this time, our price was almost four times what we'd been booked for in their town. They made lots more money because we were bigger and better known, but we only took what was originally agreed upon. They were nice people to work with and were very appreciative of how we handled it. To tell you the truth, we were a little proud, too. There are quite a few people in our business and any business who never look ahead and hope they never have to look back.

★ ★ ★ ★

We have been blessed throughout our career to be associated with good people. That goes for our fans also. Our fans are the people who cook in the backyard on Saturday, go to church on Sunday and are on time for work on Monday. This was never more apparent than in the spring of 1974. We were invited to appear at the Palomino Club in North Hollywood, California. The Palomino was a night spot that everyone who was anyone played when in the L.A. area. We had declined several times for a couple of reasons. We never played clubs and our fans didn't go to clubs, but they insisted, so we made a deal. The club would take all the drink proceeds at the bar and the Statlers would take the door receipts. It was a successful night... for us. Not for the club. Our fans showed up with their kids, no less, and bought almost zero drinks. It said a lot about their loyalty and dedication. Never underestimate the power of your followers. If they like you, you're in. But if they don't, it's all over. We always listened to our fans. They didn't always tell us what we wanted to hear but they usually told us what we needed to hear.

These dedicated people were showing up to see us in larger and larger numbers. We listened to that message and decided maybe it was time to wade on out. Our agent, Dick Blake, had a dream for us. He said we should put our own show together. He even went so far as to bring in his old friend, Shorty Lavender, who also had his own agency. They merged their two businesses and assets and their two respective top acts Tammy Wynette and the Statler Brothers. The stage was set and the line-up was agreed upon when in a meeting to finalize the plan Tammy said, "I'll do the show, but I ain't following these guys." It was a gracious thing for the First Lady of Country Music to say, because we all know she could close any show anytime. Anyway, we hired Ronnie Milsap and the three acts hit the road. It was more successful than anyone had dared to dream. We set attendance records and made a lot of friends. It was beneficial for all of us.

There has never been a female country singer who brought more pure heartfelt talent and energy to a performance than Tammy Wynette. So it seems strange that a favorite memory of her wasn't even a musical one. We began a tour in the late seventies in the Colorado Rockies. All three acts were there. Ronnie, Tammy and the Statlers. It was a special night for Tammy because she arrived in a brand new touring bus with all the bells and whistles. She was very excited and invited everyone to stop by and see her new ride. At the end of the show, we Brothers went over, knocked on the door and Tammy showed us her fancy new purchase. It was beautiful. We said goodbye and as we were walking away from the bus, we met Ronnie and his assistant. I want to remind you here that Ronnie Milsap is blind. That's the reason for his assistant, but being the jokester he is, Ronnie was going to see Tammy's new bus.

Ronnie says to me, "Harold, quick, tell me what it looks like."

I said, "Okay. It's green and tan and has light wood cabinets with beige seats."

Ronnie said, "Good. Let's go."

We followed along as he went up the bus steps and said hello to Tammy. He proceeded to comment on the earth tones and cabinet colors. Tammy put her hands to her mouth and said, "Oh, my lord," while she backed away from this blind piano player critiquing her bus design. It only took a minute for her to realize she'd been set up, but it was a long time before we let her forget it.

In time, Ronnie went off to do his own show, Tammy went on to even more success and we started to look for a new opening act. We couldn't have done better. We asked Barbara Mandrell to join our show. I don't have to tell you what a talent she is. Pick, sing, dance, and she ain't bad to look at. We played all the big buildings in all the big cities and did great business. Barbara, of course, would go on with her stellar career so after eighteen months we were looking again to find that fresh approach. This time we invited Brenda Lee to replace Barbara.

Brenda, one of my favorite people in all the world, said, "Of course I'll open for the Brothers. Milsap did and won Entertainer of the Year. Barbara did and won Entertainer of the Year. Why wouldn't I want to be Entertainer of the Year?"

Like I said, we were always blessed with good people.

Chapter Eleven

Whatever happened to Randolph Scott ridin' the trail alone
Whatever happened to Gene and Tex and Roy and Rex, The Durango Kid
O' whatever happened to Randolph Scott his horse plain as could be
Whatever happened to Randolph Scott has happened to the best of me
— Harold Reid and Don Reid
"Whatever Happened To Randolph Scott"

— Don —

We happened onto a style of songwriting in the 1970s that gave us a body of work and a public image that could never have been planned. We sang about our memories and were given credit for heading up a nostalgia craze that swept the decade. The four of us had not only gone to school together but had gone to the movies together every Saturday morning to see our Western heroes and the serials and then when we came out of the theater we'd stop at Morgan's Music Store and buy the latest Dean Martin or Ames Brothers record. So it wasn't unusual that during our traveling all over the world together that a lot of our conversation was of the 'old' days. Those memories leaked eventually into our songs and there you have it. Mix all that in with our love of the Southern Gospel quartets and when that comes out of the oven, my friend, you have the Statlers Brothers.

After moving to Mercury and winning a third Grammy®, we had full control over our albums and our singles. Jerry Kennedy, friend and producer, put the polishing touches on everything we recorded and we had the creative freedom every artist dreams of. We even took freedoms in other fields besides the recording industry. Once on location at Loretta Lynn's farm while taping a segment for Music Country, the NBC summer replacement for the Dean Martin show, we took the freedom to strip down to our underwear on national TV when the clouds opened up while we were trying to sing "Class Of '57." The director kept the tape rolling and we kept the clothes coming off so that the song couldn't be used as we looked pretty ridiculous with our hair plastered to our heads. As it was, it was such a hit with the network that the clip was shown everywhere, we were invited back for a winter shot and stripped to our long underwear in front of the Capitol in Washington D.C., and Dean had us on his show when his season started back.

But the music was never taken lightly. A single artist can make a decision to record or discard a song on a whim. When you have four men to consider, more serious measures have to be taken to make sure everyone has an equal say and is satisfied with the outcome. We developed a system early on of choosing songs. When it came time for each album, we would sit around our conference room table and each would bring songs we thought suitable for the project. Harold and Lew and I wrote, as would Jimmy later, so we would bring original material, but not necessarily. A new slant on an old song; anything was fair game. We'd listen to all the material, maybe 25 or 30 songs, and then we'd each take a list of the titles and put one to four stars beside each, according to our preference, secret ballot style. The next step then was to add up the stars. Any song that got 16 stars was a shoo-in for the album. Those with 15 and a half stars were next in line and right on down until we used up the top 10 most-voted-for titles. That was our album and we all were pleased. It worked for nearly 40 years.

Phil, not being a writer, certainly manifested his talents in another way. We all could read a little music, but Phil was the best. His parents, Elwood and Marjorie, were both very musical. They sang in the choir at church for years and Phil remembers first hearing his mother sing alto and quizzing her on what she was doing. She showed him the notes and explained what they did and he learned to harmonize by standing beside her in the pew. He had the best ear of us all and always knew what his and everyone else's part should be. Once we decided on a particular arrangement for a song, the next step was working out the harmony. The only instruments we used for these woodshed sessions around the table were a guitar or a piano. (I play just enough piano not be harmful to my health.) This was usually a rather simple process but in case anyone had trouble with a section or a chord or a note, Phil was the one we would look to. But you had to ask. His nature is such that he would never correct or even offer help unless someone specifically asked. He would never say, "You need to sing this note," unless you said, "What note do I need to sing?" A perfect example is one that happened more times than I can recount. On a song where the tenor would be singing the melody, I would sing the tenor part down an octave and Phil would sing the baritone (alto) above me. I have a tendency to 'jump parts,' meaning that sometimes I would land on the harmony note that was supposed to be his and then sometimes I wouldn't. First time through, he'd never say a word. Second time through, not even a glance. But if by the third run-through I would still be on and off his part, he'd say, "Make up your mind, D.S." And then he would proceed to grab whatever note was open. He has a great talent and flexibility for being musically fast on his feet.

★ ★ ★ ★

We made the longest trip of our lives when we moved from Columbia to Mercury and it was only across the street. We recorded our first song there September 11, 1970, and it was a song we had been pitching to everyone in town for about two years. Harold had written it and it had an unusual theme that at the time scared everyone off, so we decided to record it ourselves.

Now for some reason, the day we recorded that particular song, I was wearing an old cowboy hat. I like hats and I have a closet full of them. This certain one this certain day was not necessarily a favorite of mine; it just happened to be the one I had on at the time. We finished the session and subsequently the album and that first song was, of course, "Bed of Rose's" and it was a major hit for us. I'm not really a superstitious type of guy, however, I do tend not to challenge fate. In other words, I don't walk under a ladder just to see what will happen. I avoid the ladder without making a commitment one way or the other. I've taught a Sunday School class for over twenty years and we've had many lively discussions on the subject of faith and superstitions, so I probably shouldn't tell this on myself, but in every recording session thereafter for the next thirty-three years, I wore or carried that hat. It was always close by, hanging on a microphone somewhere. Jerry Kennedy wouldn't begin an album without asking, "Is the hat here?"

I don't have it anymore. I gave it to my son, Langdon, and he takes it to all of Grandstaff's sessions. If it could only talk, it could write a book of its own.

★ ★ ★ ★

Gospel music had been so important to us growing up. We wanted to sing like James Blackwood and The Blackwood Brothers Quartet. We wanted to perform like Hovie Lister and The Statesmen. And that is basically where our style was rooted. We sang country lyrics with gospel harmonies and no quartet had done that before, thus making us original. And we never did a concert and seldom an album without a gospel song being included. One that became associated with us was the classic Stuart K. Hine "How Great Thou Art." It was the climax to nearly every stage show we ever did, and even some TV shows.

In the early 70s we did the Phil Donahue TV show a number of times. This was when he was still having entertainers and before he went completely political. We had a nice rapport with Phil and always had fun with him and his callers and his studio audience. After doing the show a couple of times, he called us when he heard we were coming to Columbus to play the Ohio State Fair in September of '73. He said he was doing his television show from the grounds there all week long and asked if we would stop in that afternoon and say hi on the air. We did and then he asked if we would sing a song for him. When we agreed, he requested "How Great Thou Art" and to our surprise, the stage filled with the Ohio All-Youth Choir— 350 teenaged voices—which had learned our arrangement and performed this grand old hymn with us, raising the canvas roof of that gigantic circus tent at least three feet off the ground. We sang it twice!

★ ★ ★ ★

Television was becoming a big part of our lives in this decade. We did guest shots on all the major shows and even the minor ones. We plugged the records and tour dates and made the rounds to all the awards shows: CMA, Music City News, American Music Awards, Dove Awards, People's Choice Awards. Once we started winning these awards, we were invited to be presenters and then to perform. But one spot on these awards shows we had never even considered was the top spot; that of the host. A group hosting a television show? Couldn't be done. Don't even think about it.

Then enter a TV producer in Nashville, Jim Owens. We got to know Jim and hit it off as friends with him as he was as crazy into nostalgia as we were. He had his fingers into a number of TV productions and finally got a shot at producing the Music City News Awards show. He called us and asked if we would be interested in co-hosting the show with Lynn Anderson and Mel Tillis. This was a groundbreaking event for TV, country music *and* the Statler Brothers. But our attitude was, "Why not?" That began a business relationship and friendship with Jim that has lasted until this writing and I trust will endure throughout this lifetime. He and his lovely wife, Lorianne

Crook, are two of the easiest people to work with in any industry.

We hosted that particular show for nine years, winning 48 Music City News Awards and establishing ourselves as a television act. Along with Pat and Billy Galvin, we wrote our own comedy material those first couple of years and then Harold and I began writing all our routines which we had been doing for the stage shows from the beginning. On the strength of our hit records and TV acceptance, Jim wanted us to do a two-hour television special. Again, we could write it, have any guests we wanted and tape it any place we wanted. So we wrote it, got Roy Rogers, Chet Atkins, Conway Twitty, Barbara Mandrell, Brenda Lee, Janie Fricke, and taped a lot of it on location in our hometown. We now had the same artistic freedom with television that we did with records because the first special was a hit.

And so was the second one a couple of years later. My random memories kick in here with two things that stick out in my mind. On this show one of our guests was the gospel group, The Masters Five. The group consisted of our heroes from the southern gospel field, Hovie Lister, J.D. Sumner, James Blackwood and Jake Hess. They sang a song with us on the stage of the Tennessee Performing Arts Center for all the world to see but sang one just for us, in private, that no one heard but us a few months later that means more to me than I have words for. They were passing through Staunton while on tour and stopped by our office complex just to say hi. We were all standing in my office, which was rather roomy and which housed an old upright piano in the corner that I used for writing. Harold casually said, "Before you guys leave, why don't you christen Don's piano for him?" Hovie pulled out the bench, sat down, and they sang "Goodbye, World, Goodbye" and suddenly I was nine years old again and that All-Night Sing was just for me. I can still walk in there on the quietest of days and hear them and often I do.

My other random memory was of Maggie Valley, North Carolina. We went down there with the entire crew to an old Western town and shot a skit

Lew, Joe McDorman (who started it all), Phil, Harold and Peggy Smiley Desper. The first group picture ever taken of the 4 Star Quartet. 1955

"THE STATLER BROS."
SONGS AND SOUNDS OF THE STAGING STATLERS

The first publicity picture of the Statler Brothers as you knew them. Don, Harold, Phil, Lew. 1961

The Johnny Cash Show circa 1965. The Carters – Helen, Mother Maybelle, June, Anita. The Tennessee Three – Luther Perkins, W.S. Holland, Marshall Grant. John. The Statlers – Don, Phil, Harold, Lew.

The Cash troupe on stage after Carl Perkins joined us.

Don, Harold, John, Phil, and Luther Perkins backstage.

Rehearsal the night before the Folsom Prison album with John and June.

John, Carl Perkins and the Statlers rockin'.

Standing Room Only

A special moment on stage

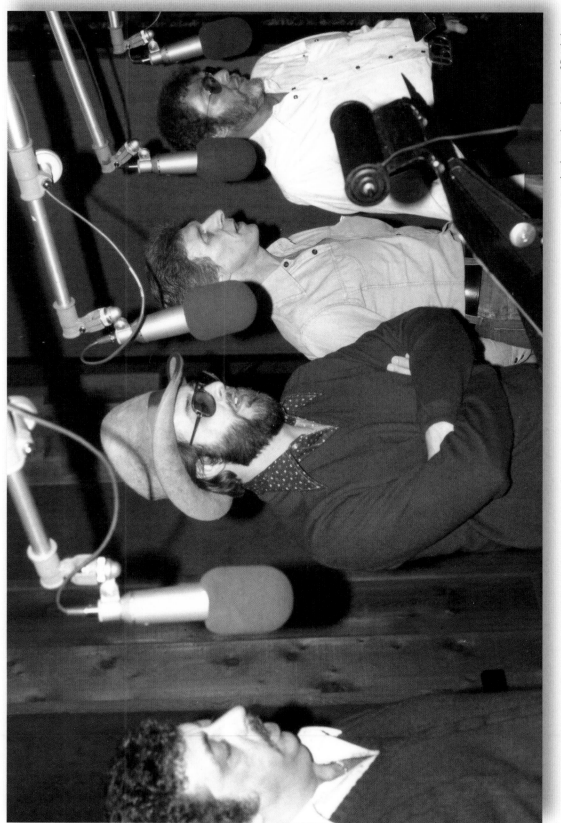

Music director Snuff Garrett, director Hal Needham, and the Great One on the set of Smokey and the Bandit II with the Statlers before the orange paint fell.

The feature act gets to do a little barbershop harmony

It was a Revolutionary idea

Roy Rogers and 4 Buckaroos

We spent a week one night on the Joey Bishop Show

Barbara Mandrell, Harold, Phil, Crystal Gayle, Minnie Pearl, Don, Lew, Chet Atkins, Grandpa Jones and Ramona.

Undressed on TV in the rain. (photo by Joe Rinehart)

With Conway and having a good time

Undressed on TV in the rain No.2 in Washington, D.C.

July 4th – Staunton, VA

Arial shot of 100,000 that converged on Staunton for the 4th of July

Our hometown named a boulevard for us

Lester 'Roadhog' Moran and His Cadillac Cowboys. Wesley (Don), Red (Phil), Wichita (Lew), Lester (Harold)

Our last appearance with Lew

Don, Phil, President Nixon, John, Lew, Harold

The night we entertained at the White House for President Sadat.

Brenda, President and Mrs. Carter, Harold

At the barbeque on the White House lawn with President and Mrs. Reagan

Don, Harold, Jimmy and Phil at a more formal affair with the First Couple

Don, Mrs. Bush, Mr. President, and Debbie.

The bus is loaded and ready to go

Another successful night at the Music City News Awards

Roy Clark, Mel Tillis, The Statlers, and John Schneider. The pretty one in the bow tie is Marie Osmond.

Dick Blake, Phil and Harold booking a tour

We four with Charlie Rose

We've worked with nearly everybody

Waiting in Hee Haw's cornfield

Harold, Don, Phil and Jimmy kicking off another Happy Birthday USA parade

Harold taking over the Ralph Emery Show

With TV producer and friend Jim Owens

They wouldn't let us drive the train. (photo by Dennis Sutton)

Our monument in Staunton. (photo by Dennis Sutton)

First Row – Chuck Norris, Jimmy, Betty White, Emmanual Lewis, LL Cool J, Oprah Winfrey, Danny White.
Second Row – Ken Dudney, Louis Mandrell, Harold, Roger Miller, Barbara Mandrell, Bob Hope, Irlene Mandrell, Sheena Easton, Don, Phil.
Third Row – Walter Peyton, John Stamos, Meatloaf, Erma Bombeck, Lynn Swann, Ron Perlman, Hershel Walker, Ron Cook.

Just to prove Don can play guitar, too. (photo by Don Putnam)

This is incorrect in more ways than politically. Video for "Let's Get Started If You're Gonna Break My Heart."

With record producer and friend Jerry Kennedy

The Mandrell Sisters – Irlene, Harold, Barbara, Don, Louise

Insert your own caption

Harold and Don on stage

Marshall Grant –
That phone is attached
permanently to his ear

Ann Peters – Our office
manager for 27 years and
friend forever

Statler Brothers and Statler Sister, Barbara Mandrell (photo by Neil Pond)

On the set with "Oh Elizabeth"

Getting ready for the cameras with Merle Haggard

Rehearsal for our weekly TNN show

Harold and Don on TV

Randy Travis

Celebrating our 30th Anniversary in show business with Lorianne Crook, June, John, and Charlie Chase

Sometimes the audience broke us up

If in doubt, pass the hat

Phil, Harold, Reba, Jimmy, and Don

Brenda Lee

With Grandstaff. Langdon & Wil. Don and Harold's sons.

Our favorite part of the TV show

Page Girls strutting their stuff

Pat Boone

TV director and friend Steve Womack (photo by Don Putnam)

With the Masters V – Steve Warren, Hovie Lister, James Blackwood, Jake Hess, and J.D. Sumner

With our buddy and favorite Sausage King, Jimmy Dean

Not just a great movie title; it's the truth (photo by Charles Clemmer)

Marshall Grant – business partner and lifelong friend

TV show in honor of WWII

Kreskin trying the impossible: to read Harold's mind

Eddy Arnold

Our musical director and Aussie buddy, Bill Walker

Saying 'Goodnight'

A tender TV moment when a little girl from the audience sang "Jesus Loves Me" to us.

Harold, Phil, Burt Reynolds, Frank Sinatra, Nancy Reagan, Donna Summer, Don, Jimmy. Now there's a stage full.

Harold and I had written for the special. It involved the four of us playing duel roles; two gangs of four having a shootout with ourselves and Mel Tillis as a cowardly sheriff and Reba McEntire as the heroine. At the time, Reba was our opening act on our concert tours, so we called her over to one of our rooms one day and told her we wanted her to do this special with us and read her the script we had written with her in mind. She was most appreciative but very honestly said she didn't think she could do it. When we pressed her for why, she confessed she had never done anything on TV and certainly no acting. She just wasn't sure she could pull it off. But we were sure and time has proven she could and did and still does every week on her own sit-com. She was as terrific then as she is now.

★ ★ ★ ★

In 1976 the Pittsburgh Steelers won their second straight Super Bowl by beating the Dallas Cowboys 21-17. After the ashes had settled and the bruises had healed, Terry Bradshaw put out the word that he wanted to sing. He had put a band together and wanted to get into country music. We thought it was a novel idea, so we booked him as our opening act in... of all places, Dallas. April 2, in front of Cowboys fans, just three months fresh from the battlefield, and he accepted the challenge. Of course, that didn't keep him from waiting on us at the back door when we arrived and sharing with us a few choice words about the whole matter. But we made it up to him. The next year we took him to Pittsburgh. But wherever he is, everybody loves Terry.

★ ★ ★ ★

Hollywood in the 70s and 80s discovered the existence of country music. Ever since Warren Beatty had sweetened the soundtrack of *Bonnie and Clyde* with Lester Flatt and Earl Scruggs, they had seen the commercial appeal of their show business cousins to the south. We had a song, "Whatever Happened To Randolph Scott," in some film called *Drive-In*. (Honestly I never saw it.) Clint Eastwood called on Nashville for help a number of times, as did Burt Reynolds. Burt called on us for the follow-up to his box office hit, *Smokey And The Bandit*, cleverly titled *Smokey And The Bandit II*. It also was a hit, but no Oscar winner. Our role was to sing two songs. One on camera, "Do You Know You Are My Sunshine," and one off camera, "Charlotte's Web," the joke being that Charlotte was an elephant being hauled cross-country so that… ah what does it matter. It was all about car wrecks and rednecks with just enough music thrown in to sell it to the yokels. We were in the opening scene, dressed resplendently in blue tailor-made and hand-stitched suits, trimmed in red and white; one of the many matching costumes we wore during that period of our career. They were, and I tell you this only for the sake of this particular story, very expensive. So after we got positioned in our scene, which was a concert sort of thing with us on stage performing, the director told us that in the middle of our song an airplane would fly over and dump bright orange paint on us. In answer to the non-reaction he received from us, he assured us Universal Pictures would pick up the cleaning bill and if that wasn't good enough they would replace the suits at any cost. Being easy guys to get along with, we agreed and continued filming.

Now switch to the other side of the set about a hundred yards away. Jackie Gleason, who was not in this scene, was leaned back in a straight chair, smoking and holding court in front of his trailer, and telling everyone who would listen what was going to happen to us. He said, "Those suits of the Statlers cost over 5,000 dollars a piece and they're going to ruin them," and on and on. Where he got his assumed information about the price we have no idea as he showed no interest in ever talking to us. We found the whole scenario rather funny afterwards, but presently we were busy getting orange paint poured over our heads by a moving aero plane. He was Mr. Show Biz and we found him more fun to observe than to interact with. *And away we go!*

It was a mess. It washed out of our hair and off our skin rather easily but an attempt at dry cleaning suggested that an orangey cast was permanently imbedded in the material. When we got home a check was waiting for us from Universal making good their promise to replace the suits, but before we did that we decided to take them to our hometown cleaners who did our cleaning after every tour. In one day and out the other and those suits were again as blue and bright as the first day we had worn them. We thanked the studio for their offer but told them for five dollars a piece we were able to get it all taken care of and sent their five-figure check back 'uncashed.' They were incredulous that we didn't take them up on their offer. They said they had never in their history had anyone return money to them and were downright baffled by our actions.

Show business people just aren't used to dealing with honest folks.

★ ★ ★ ★

The little movie skirmishes were fun, but the records and concert tours were our lifeblood. We were breaking attendance records practically every night and many times our own from previous years. Barbara Mandrell was touring with us and being followed around from city to city by TV producers who wanted her to come to Hollywood and do a series. After many talks and meetings, she decided to do just that. And we were elated for her. She did her series on NBC for two years and we went out a couple of times and guested with her. Another random memory just kicked in:

I had written a line for Harold to deliver at the end of each of our concerts. Sort of a signature sign-off. It was, "We ain't even started yet." This carried over later to our TV show, but having seen us use this line on the stage for years, Barbara called one day before the final taping of her first show and said she needed a sign-off line. I gave one that she used on every show, "I hope I have made you as happy as you've made me tonight." It was sexy, warm and sincere and she delivered it like the pro she was and still is. So while we were there taping one of her shows as guests, she decided she wanted Harold and me to dress up like her sisters and come out and do her closing with her. Sure, we'll do that. Harold with a big bushy mustache and me with a full beard and both of us in evening gowns; yeah, that'll be a good sight gag. But first we had to get fitted for the dresses, so they took us down the hall to the dress department, had us each strip down to our underwear and stood us on little round dressing islands in front of full length mirrors. Then in came two of the nicest and gayest wardrobe assistants you have ever seen and fitted us in bras and falsies. And here we stand in our brief underwear and bras with two men flitting around us saying, "Oh, I think this is going to look peachy." We just looked at one another with the same thought in mind—"Is show business really worth it?"

Chapter Twelve

Yesterday will never be forgotten,
Tomorrow's ten thousand years away
Everything we ever had together
We owe it all to yesterday
— Harold Reid and Don Reid
"We Owe It All To Yesterday"

— Harold —

We are in the only business in the world that doesn't allow you to complain about how you feel. Your preacher, your plumber, your neighbor, even your doctor can tell you how bad their head hurts or that their nose is stuffed up, but no one wants to pay big money for a concert ticket, looking to have a great night of music, comedy and lots of fun, and have someone come out and tell you not to expect too much because they have walking pneumonia. Our job was to make it look easy. Then everybody has a good time.

But to be really honest, some days were better than others. Lots of times we would drive seven or eight hundred miles just to arrive in time to dress and get on stage. In fact out West once we pulled in late and didn't even have time to change clothes before starting the show. It might be a cold, a sore throat or even the flu, but you hit the stage smiling because that's your job. Just because you feel bad you don't want the audience to feel sorry for you. When you're on a long tour, you're usually always tired. I remember one night in eastern Pennsylvania I was suffering from an inner ear infection. My physical balance was unstable and the echo from the sound system was unbearable. I know some of you will say, "It sounds like you were drunk." I'll answer that. I have never had a drink in my life. I've never even tasted beer. Neither has my brother, Don, nor my brother, Phil. We saw how it affected people and decided we could do stupid things sober and not have to wake up with a hangover. Anyway, getting there, being on time and doing your best are large responsibilities. It's not always easy when you feel good. It's even worse when you're seriously ill.

Lew had been fighting his lower stomach ailments for several years. As I told you earlier, we had to leave him in the hospital on several occasions and were forced to cancel or postpone entire tours. For many years they treated him for ulcers but finally determined it was much more serious. He was diagnosed with Crohn's Disease. It's not easy to stand by and watch a friend suffer when there's nothing you can do.

We were fortunate enough to set our tours about twelve months in advance each year. In our business, that's a blessing, but Lew came to see these blessings as obligations. Our career was our opportunity but Lew saw it as a burden. We had started years earlier to alleviate his part of the work so all he would have to do was go on stage and sing. Before we had a bus, we did all the driving; we did all the tour planning; the interviews; took care of all the business and tended to all the details that he didn't want to be involved in.

Lew always joked, "I like having a day with nothing to do and all day to do it in." Like the rest of us he was a great film fan. He collected and viewed his movies and seemed to be happy doing that. Knowing he was in constant pain, we three had promised his doctor we would work to keep all stress from him. Truthfully, it affected his whole being. You see, Lew and I had been best friends since fourth grade. We played cowboy, we carried black snake whips, we ran from killer dogs, and we imagined more ghosts than Universal Studios could produce. We double-dated together and spent many late nights talking and dreaming about our show business aspirations. Lew taught me three basic chords on the guitar. I still don't know much more than that but he developed into an excellent instrumentalist and, of course, a world class singer. So you see, as he felt worse and wanted to withdraw, we were losing a friend, a partner, a songwriter and a piece of our harmony that we'd had since the very beginning.

We were working as best we could just to help Lew perform. He felt terrible and we were stressed and very concerned. We all knew something had to be done and finally it was. On November 14, 1981, we ended a tour in Anaheim, California. We bought Lew an airline ticket so he could get home in five hours by plane rather than five days by bus. He checked into the University of Virginia hospital and after several days of tests, we cancelled our December dates for the rest of that year. We were told by Lew's new set of doctors that he needed more surgery and several months of treatment and recovery. Those blessings and obligations were now staring us in the face in the form of signed contracts for the coming year of 1982.

The four of us met and decided that finding a temporary replacement was the only answer. I fought this because I didn't want Lew to feel bad and honestly didn't want some stranger standing on the stage with us who could never fill his shoes. We were all unsure about the move, but knew we had to fulfill our commitments. Lew said we might want to check on a young singer he'd heard at a local ski lodge. We went to work and put out the word and the very first person we auditioned was the guy from the ski lodge, Jimmy Fortune. Very impressive. Good looking, great singer and an excellent guitar player who had been born and raised about forty miles from our front door. I don't know how you view this, but we knew in our hearts that God had his mighty hand on this group from day one.

We had already arranged to hold world-wide auditions in Nashville, so we had to honor that. We spent two days with tall guys, short guys, cowboys, wanna-bees and has-beens. After many hours of smiling and saying, "Don't call us, we'll call you," we sent Jimmy Fortune a plane ticket and asked him to fly down and sing with us one more time. He was the first to audition and the last. No one could come close to his considerable talent. We hired him on the spot. Then we came home and went to work. Jimmy had to learn what we were, who we were, what we expected and all the music. He is a whiz. There is no one, and I mean no one, I have ever met who can learn and retain as much and as quickly as this Nelson County boy. He had a little advantage. It's almost uncanny how similar his childhood was to our own. He had a background in gospel music and his mother and father, Bird and Dabney Fortune, had seen that he and his eight brothers and sisters had been in church and Sunday School every Sunday morning. He had been a part of country bands since boyhood so his qualifications were impeccable.

In about a four week period we had found out that Lew couldn't go back to work; we had auditioned new people; and we had hired Jimmy and rehearsed our show with him and were on our way to appear in Savannah, Georgia, on January 28, 1982. Jimmy's first night was perfect! I don't think he missed a word or a note. No one else could have done the job. So while Lew recuperated that spring and early summer, we made all our dates and Jimmy got better every night. Lew told us he was ready to come back in early June, so, of course, we offered Jimmy a permanent job with our band. Here's a little country music trivia you can watch for. We taped a guest spot on *Hee Haw* on June 4, 1982, with Lew back as part of the group and Jimmy as part of the band. It's the only time, on or off tape, that this combination ever occurred. On Monday night the seventh, we hosted the *Music City News Awards* TV show and that would be our very last appearance with Lew.

Two weeks later on June 24th Lew came to us and said, "I don't think I can do it. I want to retire." We understood and wished him well. We called Jimmy and offered him the tenor job that he had done so well for the past six months. We rehearsed once more that same afternoon in our gymnasium at our office complex. Lew was there to listen along with Jimmy's son, Little Jimmy. As we were singing, Lew walked over to Little Jimmy and asked, "What do you think about your daddy singing with those guys?" Little

Jimmy hesitated, then said, "I don't know. He's almost better than you are." We left immediately for a tour that started in Wheeling, West Virginia, the next night. We finished the weekend and went to Nashville on Monday to tape something new called a 'music video.' No one in country music had ever had a video. We were the first. It was to be the visual for our latest record, "Whatever."

Lew was an equal partner, so after all our companies and assets were evaluated, we purchased his quarter interest. We felt a little easier knowing he would never have to worry about money in his lifetime. Lew's health never stabilized to the point he could ever feel secure. Regretfully he passed away on August 15, 1990. We were in New York and were thankful we had gone to visit him just two weeks earlier. I was glad we were out of town. I don't handle these things very well. Lew knew that and I knew he would understand.

We are forever grateful to Lew and forever thankful for Jimmy. By the way, another little piece of trivia to look for; if you ever see the "Whatever" video, it's Jimmy's face and Lew's voice. We simply didn't have time to re-record it. In a way it's kind of a nice transition. For a few minutes, we had them both.

Chapter Thirteen

Carry me back and make me feel at home
Let me cling to those mem'ries that won't let me alone
Where it was always summer and she was always mine
Carry me back, Lord, while I've still got the time
—Harold Reid and Don Reid
"Carry Me Back"

— Don —

I don't think we knew at the time what we were actually living through. It was the most stressful and intensive period of our career because of all the piling-on that was about to take place. Our focus was on Statlerizing Jimmy. (That's Barbara Mandrell's word. She used to say that once a person was Statlerized on our music and concerts, they were a fan forever.) He made this as easy as possible because he always hit the stage with a smile and an energy that rang true night after night. Harold and I wrote an opening comedy routine centered around him that we used for the rest of that first year just to familiarize the fans with him and draw attention to his attributes. We held press conferences before each performance to 'present' him and answer questions about the transition. We got to the studio as soon as our schedule allowed to make sure we all recorded well together and that the Statler sound was maintained. We had a completely new wardrobe made. (Harold again. He designed all our stage clothes during the years we dressed alike.) So every minute of our lives was spoken for and planned for and there was little time for any other considerations. But just when you think you're taking care of the most essential business at hand, God often taps you on the shoulder to tell you there's something more important that needs your attention.

Less than four months after the day that Lew retired and Jimmy did his first date with us as a permanent Statler on June 25, Harold pulled in beside me on the elementary school parking lot where I was waiting to pick up my son, Langdon. He was there every afternoon picking up his son, Wil, but when he knocked on my car window and I rolled it down, I saw a look in his eyes and on his face I'd never seen before. He very matter-of-factly said, "I just came from having a checkup at the doctor's office and they want me to come in for more tests tomorrow. They think I have cancer."

For anyone who's been there, you know the world stops spinning for a long, suffering moment and then awkward words of hope spill out aimlessly as you try to find the right thing to say. That long moment stretched into uneasy days as all the preparations were made. With the help of his surgeon, Dr. Cary Buckley who has also become a good friend, we checked him into the hospital the night before under an assumed name to attract as little media and fan attention as we could. Early the next morning, October 8, 1982, he was in the O.R. and sometime about mid-morning, as his wife, Brenda, and I, and a few others sat vigil in the family room, Dr. Buckley came in, still in his scrubs, and said, "Well, we were right. He has cancer. But I think we got it all."

I can remember nearly passing out before he got to his last sentence and I had to sit down heavily after he left the room. But thank God, the worst was over. There would be radiation for a couple of weeks and a lot of rest, but we were assured he was going to be alright. (Harold and I have never since discussed this next part, but the night before the surgery, we promised one another and the Lord that when it was all over and he was out of harm's way, we would each go down to the American Cancer Society office and write them a healthy check. That next week we each did separately. Healthy ones.)

What we were threatened with was the loss of an irreplaceable brother, father, husband, and son. And I'm not even going to get into those most important areas. Let's keep it on a professional level right now and I'll try to tell you where Harold fit into the Statler Brothers organization. He was the bass singer. He was the fourth part that made us unique. There had been and were trios in country music—The Willis Brothers, The Glaser Brothers, The Gatlin Brothers, The Browns. But by having a bass singer, we were different. We were a quartet and we were not gospel and we were not backup and that made us who we were. And he was the comedian and one of the best. He's fast-witted and funny on his feet and as good as anyone in any field at controlling and holding an audience. He and I wrote comedy together for years and no matter how hilarious we thought it was sitting around the desk, he would always make it funnier with ad-libs once we got it to the stage or the TV screen.

He could do and say anything to a crowd and they would love him for it even if he was scolding them or making fun of them. There is a thing in this business called 'likeability' and if you have that you can do no wrong; and he has been triple-dipped in it. Everybody comes away from a concert loving him: little kids, adults, old women, and rednecks in spite of themselves. Here are just a few random one-liners and situations of his that I would jot down after each show, knowing that someday I'd want to remember them.

• Cleveland, Ohio, April 1975 – Faron Young, Waylon Jennings and the Statlers had two sell-out houses. The problem was that only Faron and the Statlers showed up. It was in the round and we performed on a revolving stage. When we hit the stage running, someone set the speed on 'warp' and we were going around and around so fast we could hardly keep our balance. We were laughing and the audience was laughing and Harold saved the moment by walking to the mike and saying, "If Waylon was moving this fast, he'd *be* here by now."

• The State Fair in Hutchinson, Kansas – It was an outdoor show and it was raining so hard the fair board didn't know whether to call it all off or plow through it and get it over with. The determining factor was that no one was leaving. The crowd was sitting there in their slickers and blankets with umbrellas and rain hats and no one was budging. We said, "What the heck, let's do it," so we pounced out on the platform and began singing and everyone was happy. Harold again felt compelled to take to the mike and say, "If you good people can come out here and pay your money to sit in the rain, the least we can do is come out here and take it."

• Or he'd do a non sequitur line right in the midst of a frantic routine off the top of his head. One of my favorites was, "This kind of stuff wouldn't happen if *I* was still alive." Lines like this would destroy the three of us and then the audience and sometimes we'd never get back to singing the way we should have because nothing will take away your voice quicker than laughing.

• His profanity was never really profane. It was mild and seldom but well placed when needed. One night in Battle Creek, Michigan, when a joke sort of bombed, he turned to me and said, "To hell with them. I never liked Corn Flakes® anyway."

• Or one night when we all bowed after the first song and we heard something tear and we all looked at him. He knew what had happened and he knew he had an hour to stand out there trying to cover up the obvious so he simply walked to the microphone and said, "I just ripped the whole ass out of my pants." He turned and showed them, they howled and loved him and he had nothing to worry about or cover up for the rest of the night.

• One night the stage was extremely small. With the band and all the equipment and then finding a place for the four of us out front, we were constantly tripping over cords and backing into amps between songs and it got noticeable and annoying and funny and finally as the night drew on, Harold said to the audience, "The last time I was this close to someone we had a baby."

• Phil is only 13 days older than Harold and that was just enough to provide him with all he needed to chide Phil over the years about being the "old man" of the group. It became a part of our comedy routines and also of his ad-libs. Once in New York when a little girl of about six approached the stage to give Harold a flower, he bowed down and took it and said, "Little girl, you're very pretty. You got a mother?" She shook her head yes. He said, "You got a grandmother?" Again she shook her head yes. And then he hollered over his shoulder, "Hey, Phil, she's got a grandmother."

I could fill the rest of this book with these kinds of stories but to sum it all up I'll use Harold's own words. He wrote an original maxim years ago: *When the unexpected is inevitable, counteract with the obvious.* He lived by that on stage.

I called all the band and office staff into the conference room and I told them what was taking place concerning Harold's health. I cancelled the necessary concert dates and worked to keep everything quiet and away from the press as Harold is not one to want sympathetic attention. After his treatments started, I met with his doctor and asked him exactly how long from now it would be before he could go back to work. Cary said, "That can vary. If he's strong, two more weeks."

That's all I needed to hear. I knew he was strong so I began putting everything in motion. I made all the calls Harold would have made as he was always the one who coordinated our tour plans and date schedule with our agent. I contacted all the employees and set everything and everyone on go, and exactly five weeks from the day of his surgery, he was on stage in Beaumont, Texas, beginning a 10-day tour.

This is the first time we've shared any of this with the public. We always strived to keep our personal lives out of the spotlight so that we would have some semblance of privacy and so that we could maintain a little image-control with the audience. Harold was funny and unpredictable on stage and we didn't want to do anything to alter that impact with the fans. He's been cancer-free ever since this incident and we will be eternally grateful to God for his healing hand and watchful eye.

★ ★ ★ ★

We were back on tour. Ricky Skaggs was our opening act until the first of '83 when we took on a label mate from Mercury. Jerry Kennedy, our producer, told us one day that he had just signed a new girl "who sings so great I can't tell if the songs are any good or not." And he was right. She could sing a computer manual and make you listen. So that January Reba McEntire started touring with us and things were beginning to settle in and settle down.

When we left the Cash organization back in 1972, we were staff song-writers with John's House of Cash publishing company. One of the first things we did when striking out on our own was establish our own publishing firm, American Cowboy Music Company. This was the best business move we ever made because we were writing practically everything we recorded, so this meant now we were coming at the industry in three major directions—as writers, performers, and publishers. Most people made good livings off one of these aspects, so with all three in our domain, we had found a treasure chest we couldn't lift. There just was no time to do it all, so Jerry Kennedy introduced us to one of the top publishers in Nashville by the name of Bill Hall. He was very successful and had established himself years before and was easily one of the most respected figures in the publishing business in country music. We hit it off immediately as friends and Bill agreed to manage our publishing business for us along with his many companies. This took a lot of work and with his inside knowledge we were able to expand and have other publishing businesses through the years. He managed our companies for eleven years until the spring of '83 when he suddenly had a heart attack and died.

That October, just six months later, Dick Blake, our booking agent and friend, passed away. This was the piling-on I referred to earlier. In sixteen short months, Lew retired, Harold had surgery, Bill Hall and Dick Blake, who were essential to our organization, died and we were out there performing every night like we knew what we were doing. We got through that most trying period with the help from God and each other. Thankfully Harold, Phil, Jimmy, and I were all pulling in the same direction in the same harness. Without one another I shudder to think where we might have wound up.

★ ★ ★ ★

A lot could and should be said for our organization because we had some of the best. In 1975 we were faced with needing not just a secretary but an office manager who could field phone calls and make travel arrangements and finesse their way through whatever may come in a day's time in our sometime frantic and unusual office atmosphere. For years we had dealt with a local travel agency and were impressed with a lady who handled so much of our business on a daily basis. Harold went to see her and try to talk her out of the travel business and into the show business. He succeeded and that spring Ann Peters came with us and became our right arm. She went from the only office employee to managing a staff of five and stayed with us right till the end in 2002.

Twenty-seven years as a friend and a colleague and never a cross word or a problem. Ann not only knows where all the bodies are buried, she knows who killed them.

Over the years she kept together a wonderful and loyal staff that answered our fan mail, published our newsletters, booked interviews, produced tour schedules, kept our books and payroll in order and changed last minute plans with nary a huff or a puff. We must mention her staff of ladies through the years and our thanks for all they did in keeping the home office afloat: Doris Critzer, Mariann Van Buren, Ginny Lowe, Janet Linen, Shirley Chittum, Cathey Morton, Betty Lancaster, and Dot Gilchrist.

On tour, where Marshall Grant was our right arm, the counterpart to our office staff was our band. Throughout our career we only had twelve different musicians: Darryl Mizer, Lee Flory, Don "Mousey" Morton, Tommy Floyd, Carroll Durham, Jerry Hensley, Charlie Hamm, Billy James, Scott Cash, Terry Lafon, Vaughn Thomas and Tommy Starnes. And maybe the most important people who held our trust and our lives in their very hands every day and night were the bus drivers: Dale Harman, Mike Wilkins, and the Eckard brothers, Stuart and Charlie. There were also numerous sound and light crews who traveled a half-a-day ahead of us and set up all that equipment every afternoon and then tore it down every night. They had the hardest and least appreciated job of any of us on the road. You hardly ever see a roadie over forty years old. It's a young man's game.

More and more the business end was taking over our lives. We were constantly faced with as much conference room time as we were bus time and hotel room time. It's strange how little of his life a performer spends on stage (maybe an hour and half a night) and how much is spent on all the other features of the business. But we learned early on that those who didn't take care of the business side awoke one day to find that it was gone. No more goose—no more eggs. So we took care of the goose.

Our attorneys and CPAs and advisors had us into things we never dreamed of. We owned coal mines in West Virginia, nursing homes in New Jersey and petroleum companies in Oklahoma as tax shelters. We were invested in restaurant chains and mobile homes and rental properties and were fed reports and figures that we had no desire to eat, when along comes a man who would shoulder the hard-core, day-to-day business concerns for us and become a close and personal friend—our CPA and business advisor, R.G. "Butch" Hupp. To this day we're with him weekly and depend on him for anything that has a number in it, on it or anywhere near it.

Our Washington attorney through a lot of those years was Bill Utz who shared our love and hobby of collecting the old western movies. Our Staunton attorney was and still is Wick Vellines whose knowledge of the law is surpassed only by his ability to recite the dialogue to every Marx Brothers film ever made. And our Nashville attorney who was responsible for putting together the deal for this book you're reading is Russ Farrar who is as big a Southern Gospel fan as we are. So you can see we always marry our business with a dash of pleasure. It makes the medicine go down a little easier.

And that was the Statler organization. We had followed the advice of our old mentor, Johnny Cash, who used to say to us, "Always surround yourself with good people." We had some of the best.

★ ★ ★ ★

Back on stage, we were rockin' right along. We decided to give Las Vegas a try so we began headlining there from time to time. Speaking for myself and Jimmy, I think we enjoyed the change, but Harold and Phil never got used to sitting in one place for a week at a time. Although we were very successful there, we didn't go back much after the first year or so as there was plenty of concert work available throughout the USA and the one-night-stands had sort of gotten into our blood. We did spend a week in Omaha in March of '84 at an event called Aksarben. (That's Nebraska spelled backward for all you folks with 'tired blood.' You won't catch that unless you actually remember the *Lawrence Welk Show*.) Aksarben was a hundred-year-old festival put on by the state and we were booked there for twelve shows in six days and it was sold out weeks in advance. Therefore any opening act we may want to take with us need not be of any marquee value, so we became open to anyone looking for a job. We were pitched a new duo who was trying to get a start in Nashville and decided they would be a good choice. They were a mother and daughter act and called themselves simply The Judds. They were green and scared to death but charming and talented and willing to work. Wonder whatever happened to them?

★ ★ ★ ★

We had some terrific opening acts such as Marie Osmond and Janie Fricke. One was a young man from Carolina who came over and spent time with us on the bus and showed a lot of character both on and off the stage. Randy Travis was on his way and we knew it. Another was a guy who had been knocking around Music City for a few years and had even done some demo sessions for us for our publishing company. We liked his singing and took him out with us for a short tour. The only problem was that our audience complained constantly about how loud his music was. We didn't say much to him about it as we felt that was his business and he could deal with the people however he wanted to. And I'm glad he didn't give in and turn down for if he had, the world may never have discovered the Garth Brooks they came to know and love.

★ ★ ★ ★

Another, a few years before, was a great new talent that was being pushed and promoted by his record company. They were about to release an album on him and called us and asked if we would consider taking him on tour with us as we were about to launch across Canada for a three-weeker. When the question of money came up, they quickly said, "No. There's no money involved. We'll take care of paying him and his expenses." So we said, "Sure. What have we got to lose?" And the answer to that was emphatically, "Nothing," because we got a fresh, new Eddie Rabbitt as our opening act—free and clear.

★ ★ ★ ★

My favorite opening-act-story comes straight from the act herself. She tells it on stage to this very day and she remembers it exactly the way we do.

I was watching the *Crook and Chase* TV show one afternoon at home in late 1987 and was completely taken by a young, pretty, unknown singer who just stood there with a guitar and no band and sang and played the old Fats Waller song, "Ain't Misbehavin'." The performance was hypnotic. The next day at the office I told my Brothers about her and then called Jim Owens, our good friend who produced the C&C show, and had him send us a clip from the previous day's show of this multi-talented girl singer. We were all so impressed that we told Marshall to get in touch with her and put her on a concert someplace so we could see her in an on-stage situation.

The first available date we had open to book her was in March of '88 in Plant City, Florida, at the Strawberry Festival. It was an outdoor show with thousands of people seated and standing for as far as you could see. She took the stage and did her set while we stood by and watched, enjoying everything she did. And then as she finished and was about to take her final bow, a warm gust of seasonal wind blew across the stage and blew her dress up and over her head. And, as she tells the story, "I came off stage and the Statlers immediately hired me for 50 more dates." And I can't refute any of that story. That was our introduction to Suzy Bogguss.

★ ★ ★ ★

Before we get too far away from the subject of 'organization' and taking care of business, we made a major career decision in early '83 concerning our on-stage image. We went from the standard-dressed-alike-quartet-look to dressing as individuals. We all wore sport coats and dress pants, but we chose our own wardrobe and dressed more to our respective likings. The first night was March 23 in Murray, Kentucky, and I tell you this not because it has any historical value, but to express how much detail we tended to in every aspect of our business. I have kept a record of the clothes we wore on every appearance, concert or TV show, since we began singing. I've kept a record of the songs we sang on each date and the comedy routines we used. The reason was so that when we went back into an area, we could be fresh in every way. Harold has in his files every contract for every appearance with terms and riders and money. Phil can offer you files of every concert played and how many people attended and how much money was grossed, expended, and netted. Organization starts at the top and we never asked for anything we weren't willing to give.

Chapter Fourteen

There're questions we're always hearing, everywhere we go
Like how do I cut a record or get on a country show
Well, it takes more than just ambition and three chords on an old guitar
There're a few more things you gotta learn to be a country star
—Harold Reid and Don Reid
"How To Be A Country Star"

— Harold —

"Life is like Halloween; you can be anything you want if you wear your costume well." That quote pretty much sums up most people's lives. We all have to change 'hats' from one part of our life to another. Everyone wears their 'work hat,' but on the way home each day you change to your 'home hat.' We're no different than the butcher, the baker or the candlestick maker. It's just that some days it's easier to change that hat than others. If you don't change when you're supposed to, you're as out of place as a corduroy tuxedo.

Entertainers tend to become what their public wants them to be: carefree, fun-loving, and always 'up' and in a good mood. That's great! It's the way it should be, but when you get home it's time to take out the trash, drive the kids to school and mow the grass. That's great, too. But it's an adjustment.

There's a little secret I'll share. There have been nights on stage when we sang two complete songs and I didn't even remember what they were. I was thinking about one of the kids back home who had gone to the doctor that day or a piano recital I was missing at that very hour or even a fight I'd had that afternoon on the phone with someone I loved. Right place—wrong hat.

It also works the other way. I'm at a Wal-Mart shopping with my family, trying to keep up with three or four kids, well aware I'm supposed to smile and be pleasant with everyone who makes eye contact. Someone stops me, wants an autograph and tells me a long, long story about an operation their mother-in-law had before she passed away ten years ago. I grope for the right words, sign my name, but they go off feeling cheated because they feel they didn't have my full attention. They simply caught me with the wrong hat on.

We worked really hard to remain hometown and not to become something we weren't. That doesn't mean that people didn't treat us different. A neighbor we'd known all our lives was very offended because he tried to sell us four kinds of insurance the very first week of our career. He thought we had hit the lottery and were instant millionaires so he should sell us something. We simply said, "No thanks." He was looking at us in a brand new light. Hard feelings? Sure, but of course, it was our fault.

We had a dear friend once who thought we should hire him as a bus driver. We pointed out to him he had never driven a bus. He said, "I'll learn as I drive." He was a little let down when we declined his generous and very dangerous offer. He would understand Greyhound's refusal, but thought *we* should have taken the chance.

To be fair, sometimes I didn't change hats as quickly as I should have. We'd go out on a week-long tour, have sellout crowds, the number one song in the nation and have to be escorted to and from the bus by security, and wind up being a little proud of what was happening in our lives. But then back home, in a grocery store, a pretty young girl would approach me and say, "Excuse me. Aren't you Kim's father?"—that's how you stayed grounded.

Having the great fans and the wonderful things that happened to us in our career usually made it easy to put on our show-face. It was never easier than when we had lots of help. For instance, we were invited to appear with the Dallas Symphony Orchestra. Our old friend, Bill Walker, flew to Texas, rehearsed and conducted for us and we were all carried away with the quantity and quality of the music.

One of the most memorable experiences was being invited to Washington, D.C., to perform with the Air Force Symphony. It was close enough to home that we were able to take the wives and kids. The things we always worried about with having our families with us were their security and treatment. We worried about everything from one of them being snatched to some doorman not letting them backstage. These were the least of our concerns that Easter weekend in D.C. We all toured the city, visited the White House, were welcomed at the Pentagon and had to leave the Smithsonian way too soon. The Air Force personnel still found time to throw a surprise birthday party for my son, Wil. If that weren't enough, we appeared in Constitution Hall on Sunday afternoon with a world-class orchestra and 'raised the roof' as they say. It was up-lifting, inspiring, and gratifying. All that combined with an early spring ice storm made for a memorable weekend for four hillbillies from the Shenandoah Valley.

★ ★ ★ ★

Sometimes our chosen profession seems a little sad when you peek backstage. Example: We were in Lethbridge, Alberta, Canada, on Halloween night 1979. The gremlins taught us a lesson that evening. We weren't exactly 'sold out.' There're a couple of things you don't fool with when planning a tour, like kids' holidays and high school football. Don't book the show 'cause you ain't gonna win. Anyway, on this kids' holiday we had our buses parked inside the arena. Barbara Mandrell was the first half of our show and her bus was parked alongside ours. Before the music started there was a knock at our bus door. It was Barbara's daughter, Jamie, who had knocked on the only friendly door in sight. She was in her costume with her trick or treat bag. It was the only stop for a four-year-old who was 2,000 miles away from home. Sometimes it's lonesome out there.

But then sometimes it's not lonesome enough. Here's a short list of things I dreaded.

1. Sitting in a restaurant knowing eighteen people have recognized you and each of them is waiting for the other one to approach you for an autograph. You see, it's easier if you ain't the first one to ask.

2. Taking a picture and posing with three strangers while the fourth one fumbles with a camera she's never seen before. I'm hollering, "Hurry up," and the large one who forgot to bathe is hugging my left arm and saying, "Take your time."

3. Walking into a truck stop; a trucker stops you and grants himself five guesses as to who you are and wants you to wait till he can call his wife on the phone so she can talk to you. His universal comment is, "Oh, God, my wife ain't gonna believe this." Some days neither do I.

4. And last but certainly not least, the autograph request from someone who is obviously glad to see me, excited to have run me down, and is squealing at the top of her voice but assures me that she is not a fan but has chased me two city blocks to get something signed for her sister-in-law. When I start to write and ask the sister-in-law's name, the answer is usually, "just make it to me." I've always been proud to have fans. I've never understood why they were ashamed to be one.

★ ★ ★ ★

As things got bigger and better and we got more visible, it was becoming almost impossible to maintain any privacy at our hotels. All day and night the phone would ring for a large variety of reasons. It was everything from someone wanting free concert tickets to wanting to borrow money to wanting to tell you their troubles or to just be able to say they had gotten you on the phone. We were finally forced to direct all calls to Marshall's room. This proved to not only keep Marshall up all night, but to drive him nuts, also. So we worked out a system. We registered under assumed names that only our families and closest friends were privy to. You want to know now what they were? Well, of course, I'll tell you. It'll keep you from calling Marshall's room.

Jimmy's hotel name was Dabney Bird. That would be his father's first name and his mother's middle name. Phil was Lee Fielding. Now this was a little more scientific because it combined a nick name of his father with his mother's maiden name. Are you following all this? Don chose the very bizarre title of Friday Spellman. Why? I have no earthly idea. All I know is after a year he changed it to Joe Zirk. If I told you anymore I'd be violating my security clearance. And from the very first I was Wil Sidney; my son's and my father's names, respectively. It was so 'high-tech' that sometimes I had to look at our personal hotel list and mark my room in red just to know who I was.

It ain't just lonesome. It gets crazy out there.

★ ★ ★ ★

Most everyone knows by now that my baby brother, Don, and I have a lot of writing credits together. We've written songs, television specials, a television series for seven years, stage shows and just plain ol' jokes. In fact, we're writing this book together, but I guess you knew that. We've been very blessed. I've often thought that if one of us had made it in the music business while the other one stayed behind working in a grocery store, how very different our relationship would be.

I can speak for Don or at least speak about him. He could do it all by himself and without much effort. He's disciplined, tasteful and has the work ethic of a beaver. He comes away from most conversations with a song or story idea and thinks nothing of working on Saturday nights or Christmas

115

Day. He's that committed.

I have thought for years that as a songwriter he's yet to be discovered. The Statler Brothers have Don Reid songs hidden away on albums that are far and away better than most artists release as singles. I'll give you an example. We recorded a song he wrote titled "The All-Girl-All-Gospel Quartet." It's a story song (one of his specialties) and combines fiction, fact, memories and a keen sense of literature while recalling our early aspirations and our early inspirations. It's the way the craft is done when done right. It's my favorite Don Reid song and I've got a long list. Lots of them bring a tear to my eye. This one makes me cry. He has written two hundred thirty-eight (238) songs that have been recorded and even I don't know how many he has tucked away I haven't heard. Then there're books, poetry, and verse that should be studied in school. He's my brother, so I would expect him to be brilliant, but after all . . .

Now here is the part I hate to confess. We've worked hard for many years to make me the funny one. People don't realize Don and I share a sense of humor that we probably inherited from Mom. Our mother, until the day she died, could turn a phrase and find the humor in most every situation. But back to Don. He has written some great stuff and let me get the laugh. He has fed me lines on stage. He thinks funny but his ego never needed stroking. If it worked for the Statlers, it worked for him. I feel the same way, so we tried never to change something that wasn't broke. We all got a laugh when we could, but never tramped on the other one doing it.

For instance: the Country Music Awards in 1973. We won Group of the Year. Johnny Cash was hosting the show. We were there with our wives. We never wrote acceptance speeches because we never took it for granted we'd win. They announced our name, we walked up to the mike and Don thanked John for our success, then said, "We'd like to thank four very lovely ladies who are with us tonight who have given a lot more for this than we ever have." And I said, "We just hope our wives don't find out about them."

Now that's just a natural 'Groucho' response, but the audience thought it was hilarious. That's a Harold example. Here's a Don example.

It's three years later at the CMA Awards. Willie and Waylon had teamed up and managed to win three categories. Waylon was absent, so Willie had run on the stage (well, to Willie it was running) each time and accepted by saying, "On behalf of me and ole Waylon, thank you." Obviously Willie didn't write speeches ahead of time either.

They get to our category and they announce the Statler Brothers as winners. We go up to the stage and Don simply leans down and says, "On behalf of us and ole Waylon…" That's all he ever got out. The audience loved it, but it was spontaneous and confident from my brother who knew the nano second before he said it, that it would work. Our very good friend, Sonny James, told us one time that he loved to see us win just to hear what we would say.

Anyway, that is another layer of how important Don was to our organization. I remember when the draft board called him up during the Viet Nam war. He left the tour and flew home for his physical. It was a large set of problems. Don was, from the first day, an irreplaceable part of the group. He had musical talent, writing talent, organizational skills and just because he was the baby member didn't make him any less important. So when Uncle Sam called, we didn't know what to pray for. The patriotism we'd always bragged about was real, so going to Canada wasn't an option. The career that was just starting to take off was very important to all of us. The truth is, I was dealing with more than all that. It was my brother and I didn't want to share him with anyone, especially Uncle Sam. Don flew back to the tour with the news. Good or bad? We couldn't tell for sure. They had turned him down, relief and hooray, but the doctors discovered he had a condition called paroxysmal auricular tachycardia. In other words, heart palpitations.

Don had noticed, since his teen years, an occasional lightness and unusual heart rhythm in his chest and it got increasingly worse as time went by. We started meeting with doctors and found it could be somewhat controlled with small amounts of medication but the palpitations may still occur and have to be dealt with immediately when they did. Whenever Don was tired, excited or in a stressful situation, it was more likely to be set off. His heart rate would rise to about one hundred eighty (180) plus, rather than the normal seventy. We had been instructed to have him lie down and relax as best he could and I was to put pressure on the artery in his neck to suppress the blood flow and stop the increased surge. Does that sound simple? Well, it gets a little tough when you're on stage. If it happened as we were going off, we could rush backstage, lay him down and usually get it stopped. Sometimes it was on to a local hospital. Sometimes it would happen at the beginning of a concert and Don could step back during a bow and get it stopped. Sometimes it would happen halfway through a show. We could always tell. His breathing was shallow, he became very pale and he would break into a cold sweat. Unlike me, when Don starts to sweat, something is wrong.

The condition became worse as time went on. Not more often, but more severe when it happened. We were in Fort Worth, Texas, on January 23, 1999. We couldn't get it stopped without professional help, so on February 11, 1999, he underwent surgery at the University of Virginia hospital to correct the problem. He's never had another occurrence.

To us Don is indispensable. He keeps records of everything. All those years on the road he maintained a diary that showed where we were, what we sang, what clothes we wore, what jokes we told and what movie we saw if we had a night off. He's first my brother and then my business partner. He's first my inspiration and then my writing partner. I'm glad neither of us had to stay behind in that grocery store because I wouldn't have wanted to do it without him, or more truthfully, I don't think I could have done it without him. I'm glad I didn't have to try.

Chapter Fifteen

Some I wrote for money, some I wrote for fun
Some I wrote and threw away
And never sang to anyone
One I wrote for momma, and a couple still aren't through
I lost track of all the rest but the most I wrote for you
— Harold Reid and Don Reid
"Some I Wrote"

— Harold —

They say there's a story in every man so there must be one in every song. No two are alike (we hope) and no two are ever written or inspired in the same manner. Here is a list of songs you'll remember and maybe some you've never heard of. That's why we're writing this book—so we can tell you stuff you didn't already know.

So sit back and throw another log on our literary campfire and prop up your feet. Here's a little lyrical history we hope you enjoy.

— Don —

"DO YOU REMEMBER THESE?" - This idea was given to us by our publisher at the time at House of Cash. Knowing our passion for nostalgia, he thought this would be right up "Allen's Alley." (A little radio humor for those old enough to remember and that is precisely what this song was about—what you remembered.) But Harold and I were writing about things we *didn't* remember. We listed items and people and events from the decades of the 30s, 40s, and 50s and we just weren't around for all those decades but we loved the history of it all. And when we got through we had enough material not just to write a song but to write an entire album. Our biggest problem was editing it down to a three-minute single.

A song with no plot, no message and no love angle—just a laundry list of memories? Anyone in the music business in their right mind (oxymoron) would tell you it was impossible for it to become a hit but everyone related to it and it was the fastest rising song we ever had. Just six weeks after its release date it had rushed to the top of the charts. But not in England. "Over there" they had a little problem with it that we never foresaw. "Over there" it seems that one of the lines got us banned from the BBC and it was the line, "knickers to your knees." "Over there" knickers are women's panties.

Seems pretty mild for today doesn't it?

Do You Remember These?

Saturday morning serials, chapters one through fifteen
Fly paper, penny loafers, Lucky Strike Green
Flattops, sock hops, Studebaker, Pepsi please,
Ah, do you remember these?
Cigar bands on your hand, your daddy's socks rolled down
Sticks-no-plugs, and aviator caps with flaps that button down
Movie stars on Dixie Cup tops and knickers to your knees.
Ah, do you remember these?

The Hit Parade, grape Tru-Ade, the Sadie Hawkins Dance
Pedal pushers, ducktail hair and peggin' your pants
Howdy Doody, Tutti-Frutti, the seam up the back of her hose

Ah, do you remember those?
James Dean, he was keen, Sunday movies were taboo
The Senior Prom, Judy's mom, Rock and Roll was new
Cracker Jack prize, stars in your eyes, ask Daddy for the keys
Ah, do you remember these?

The boogie man, lemonade stand and takin' your tonsils out
Indian burn and wait your turn and four foul balls—you're out
Cigarette loads and secret codes and savin' Lucky Stars
Can you remember back that far?
To boat-neck shirts and fender skirts and crinoline petticoats
Mum's the word and dirty bird and a double root beer float
Moon hub caps and loud heel taps and he's a real gone cat
Ah, can you remember that?

Dancing close, Little Moron jokes and cooties in her hair
Captain Midnight, Ovaltine and the Whip at the county fair
Charles Atlas course, Roy Rogers' horse, and only the Shadow knows
Ah, do you remember those?
Gable's charm, froggin' your arm, loud mufflers, pitchin' woo
Going steady, Veronica and Betty, white bucks and Blue Suede Shoes
Knock, Knock Jokes—who's there?—Dewey—Dewey who?
Do we, remember these? Yes, we do
Ah, do we, do we remember these.

Words and Music – Harold Reid, Don Reid, Larry Lee

— Harold —

"CLASS OF '57" – Most people assume that Don and I wrote this because it was the year I graduated from high school. You're half right. Don called me one evening and said, "Let's get together and write tonight." I said, "You know, I'm tired, but let me check the TV schedule and if there's nothing on to watch, I'll call you back."

I checked. There was nothing on of interest, but one thing caught my eye. *Ironsides* had an episode that night titled "Class of '57." I called my brother and said, "Come on down. I've got an idea." Once we started writing, it became my class. Not all, but some. You remember Peggy who played piano for us. She's in there. Jerry drove the truck for Sears; Tommy sold used cars; and Freddie took his life. All true. Near the end we wrote a line that read "Judy married me," but after arranging it, I wound up singing that line so I changed it to "Brenda married me." I wanted to do that for her plus I didn't have a good explanation about who Judy was.

We received our third Grammy® for this performance. Don and I remember to this day it's the only time we ever got together to write and came away with three complete songs. Sure I'll tell you. The other two were "1953-Dear John-Honky Tonk Blues" which was recorded in great fashion by Dave Dudley and "A Special Song For Wanda" which we put on our album *Country Symphonies In E-Major*. We need to get together more often and lay off the TV.

Class of '57

Tommy's sellin' used cars, Nancy's fixin' hair
Harvey runs a grocery and Margaret doesn't care
Jerry drives a truck for Sears, and Charlotte's on the make

And Paul sells life insurance and part time real estate
Helen is a hostess, Frank works at the mill
Janet teaches grade school and probably always will
Bob works for the city and Jack's in lab research
And Peggy plays organ at the Presbyterian church

And the Class of '57 had its dreams
We all thought we'd change the world with our great works and deeds
Or maybe we just thought the world would change to fit our needs
The Class of '57 had its dreams

Betty runs a trailer park, Jan sells Tupperware
Randy's on an insane ward and Mary's on welfare
Charley took a job with Ford, Joe took Freddy's wife
Charlotte took a millionaire and Freddy took his life

John is big in cattle, Ray is deep in debt
Where Mavis finally wound up is anybody's bet
Linda married Sonny, Brenda married me
And the class of all of us is just part of history

And the Class of '57 had its dreams
But livin' life day to day is never like it seems
Things get complicated when you get past eighteen
But the Class of '57 had its dreams

Words and Music – Harold Reid and Don Reid

— Don —

"SO MARY COULD MAKE IT HOME" – This was an album song, never a single, but a perfect example of how an idea is born and developed. I spent a lot of time in my backyard playing ball when my two sons, Debo and Langdon, were growing up. We'd play till dusk most evenings and most of the neighborhood kids would join us. One summer evening a little girl from next door, Mary, had gotten on third base and it was Debo's turn to bat and he said just before I tossed him the ball, "I'm going to hit it way out in left field so Mary can make it home."

Wow! The chills came over me and I knew there was a song about to surface. As soon as he'd hit the ball, I excused myself for a few minutes and rushed into the house and to the piano and wrote the song in minutes. It was as if it gushed out of me and all from an innocent remark from a child playing a game. You never know from whence the next idea is coming.

So Mary Could Make It Home

From the first day school let out each summer, all the kids would come
To our backyard and we'd play ball and keep count of our homeruns
And all the boys would do just fine, but one thing was never known
I sacrificed my backlot average, so Mary could make it home

So Mary could make it home, so Mary could make it home
I always hit to the right fielder's mitt so Mary could make it home

Well, Mary was the first girl I ever knew to have a paper route
I taught her how to fold 'em up and how to throw 'em out
And I remember a thousand evenings when the rain would start to come

I'd finish the block and get soakin' wet so Mary could make it home
So Mary could make it home, so Mary could make it home
My old Schwinn was a rusty sin so Mary could make it home

Well, I held hands and carried books like all the other kids
But I held and carried Mary's more than anyone did
And when Mary's daddy said, "Eleven o'clock" in that low curfew tone
Well, I missed the ends of more good movies, so Mary could make it home

So Mary could make it home, so Mary could make it home
I missed the end of "Gone With The Wind" so Mary could make it home

It must have been fifteen years since we had seen each other
But a few months ago I ran into Mary and we had lunch together
We laughed and talked and then we cried and she asked if I would phone
I lied and said I'd better not so Mary could make it home

So Mary could make it home, so Mary could make it home
Now the love we steal is short but real so Mary can make it home.

Words and Music – Don Reid

— Harold —

"I'LL GO TO MY GRAVE LOVING YOU" - Now this one is a little complicated. I'm not even sure I understand it. Okay, here goes. Don wrote this song but with a very slow, love song sort of tempo. One morning, very early, between Little Rock and Memphis, I was driving the bus when Don got out of his bunk, came up to keep me company and brought a guitar along. He started to sing his slow song with a little beat. I started singing the little aftertime rhythm part and all of a sudden it caught fire. That's the way we recorded it and time has proven it was a pretty good idea.

A couple of years later I wrote a gospel lyric to the same melody which was "He Went To The Cross Loving You." So to sum it up, Don wrote 100% of "I'll Go To My Grave Loving You" but when I wrote "He Went To The Cross Loving You," I was in for 50% because it was Don's melody but my words but I didn't have anything to do with "I'll Go To My Grave Loving You." Well, I told you in the beginning I didn't think I understood it.

I'll Go To My Grave Loving You

I'll go to my grave loving you. I'd give all I've saved loving you
And should I live again, even then it won't end
For I'll go to my grave loving you

Oh, to take his place forever, there's nothing I wouldn't give
I'd prove to you daily what a man really is

I'd lay down my life loving you. I'd work day and night loving you
And when life called us both above, honey, you'd know that you'd been loved
For I'll go to my grave loving you

Words and Music – Don Reid

He Went To The Cross Loving You

He came in this world loving you. He lay in a manger loving you
He was born a babe to die a man, sacrificed to fill a plan

And He went through his life loving you
He taught the gospel truth loving you. He healed the lame and sick loving you
And when they found Him free from sin, He was crucified by earthly men
But He went to the cross loving you

To save the world forever, there's nothing He didn't give
It took Jesus Christ to show us what love really is

He laid down His life loving you. He died on the cross loving you
Two dark days passed while he was gone, but on the third he rose at dawn
And He'll come back again loving you
Because He went to the cross loving you

Words – Harold Reid, Music – Don Reid

— Don —

"YOU'VE BEEN LIKE A MOTHER TO ME" - I wrote this song for one of our Fourth of July concerts in our hometown. As it begins, you think it's a 'mother' song and it's not until about the fourth verse that you realize it's a patriotic song and toward the end there's a verse that says, "America, stand up and show it; that you're proud of the red, white and blue. You love her and you know it, 'cause she's been like a mother to you." We sang it a lot in the 80s in concert but never more memorably than when we sang it on September 23, 1981, on the lawn of the White House.

We had been invited to one of President Reagan's barbeques in the nation's front yard and were asked to entertain. A casual affair, the President showed up in a red turtleneck sweater and a green plaid sport coat. He and Nancy and the cabinet and varied senators and their wives actually were in a picnic kind of mood. So nearing the end of our show, we broke into this song and when we got to the line, "America, stand up and show it," I don't have to tell you who the first person was to hit his feet. The chills up my back and the tears in my eyes and the catch in my throat almost caused me to stop singing. Here was the President of the United States standing at attention with his hand on his heart and everyone else following suit. After three encores that night, he came to the stage and said, "You all are pretty darn good for eastern boys." I said, "But we wore our cowboy boots," and he said, "I've got mine on, too." And there's a picture someplace of all five of us standing on one foot, holding up our pants leg to show off our boots.

I don't remember word for word everything everyone has ever said to us, but I have a record of what the President said to us that night on stage. And it means enough to me to share it with you here. He said, "We have not only been extremely entertained here tonight, but we have been inspired. The "lady" they sang about is very important to us all. Sometimes we cross state lines and party lines, but we all must try to talk to each other and not *about* each other." And as he and the First Lady turned to walk down the steps of the stage, he turned back to us and said privately, "Anytime you're in the area, I'll be at the show."

And we saw him a number of times after that, but that's for another chapter.

You've Been Like A Mother To Me

She's seen me through lots of trouble; she's stayed up nights so I could sleep
She's given me more than comfort; she's given me something I can keep

I love her and I need her and I want to be with her all the time
I'd fight just to keep her and I'd die if I thought she wasn't mine

I love her every morning; thank God for her every night

I worship the ground she stands on and I stand on the grounds she'll be alright
When you need me, you know I'll be there 'cause you've always been there for me
America, God knows I love you, 'cause you've been like a mother to me

America, we've been through troubles, and we'll make it again just wait and see
America, God knows I love you, 'cause you've been like a mother to me

America, stand up and show it, that you're proud of the red, white and blue
You love her and you know it, 'cause she's been like a mother to you.

Words and Music – Don Reid

— Harold —

"THE STATLER BROTHERS QUIZ" - This one started out as a musical way to answer all the everyday questions we were asked. That's a pretty simple approach, but my brother and I took it a step further. We wrote all the questions in a verse and never gave any of the answers till we got to the chorus. Why, you ask? I don't know. It was late, we were tired and on any other given day we probably would have thrown it in the trash can. All I can tell you is that it's different and honestly I've never heard another song written in this particular form. Listen to it sometime. It ain't bad!

The Statler Brothers Quiz

These are some questions that people ask the most
So we thought we'd answer and try to come as close
To the truth of the matter, what ever the matter is
First some questions, then some answers, from The Statler Brothers Quiz

129

Are you all really brothers? Where did you get your name?
Did you all really undress on TV in the rain?
Where can I get your albums? Does Lew ever smile?
Would you listen to a song I wrote? I think it's just your style

No. From a box of tissues. Down to our underwear. Try a record store.
Yes, but only when he's sleeping. Of course, it never hurts to hear one more.

Do your wives ever travel with you on the road?
  Did you fall out with ole Johnny?
And does Harold really sing that low?
Whose class was '57? That was my year, too.
And can I have my picture taken with all four of you?

Sometimes. No, we're not mad at Johnny.
  Yes and even lower and sometimes out of key.
Harold was the kid from '57. Sure, if you can find the other three.

Which of you guys are brothers? Remember me from last year?
And why did you all ever let Donnie grow that beard?
Would you do "The Roadhog" and "Flowers on the Wall?"
And how many children do you have in all?

Harold and Don. Of course, we remember.
  To make up for what he's losing on the top.
I doubt it and yes, we always do it. Fourteen and it's probably time to stop.

Where are you all from? How much money do you get?
Is Phil always that quiet? He's so nice and kind I'll bet.
Do you still enjoy singing and traveling around?

And hey, just one more question, will you come back to our town?
Virginia. It's none of your business. Don't let his looks deceive you,
  you should hear him on the bus.
Yes, we love what we're doing. And thanks to all of you for asking us.
Thanks to all of you from all of us.

Words and Music – Harold Reid and Don Reid

— Don —

"FLOWERS ON THE WALL" - Lew DeWitt wrote this song and the story is really his; but in his absence I'll tell you about it.   He wrote the verses to the tune of "Jingle Bells." Try it and you'll see that it works. This is how we first heard it when he originally sang it to us. The chorus was to the tune of an old Crosby and Hope ditty from a 'Road Movie,' but then he reworked it and gave it a complete musical overall.   The lyric in reference to Captain Kangaroo was a natural hook as was the bass line. Usually the bass does an aftertime but in this case Harold hit the note *before* we did. All this, with the banjo and the abrupt stops, made it an ear-catching sound in both the country and pop fields.

Lew's intention was to write a song about a guy who was so lonely that he would sit in his room and count the flowers on the wallpaper just to have something to do; so bored that he would play solitaire with a deck of 51 cards knowing he could never win; and so completely out of sync with reality that he was actually watching the Captain and Mr. Greenjeans on TV. But then after it hit, the critics and the times wanted to call it the first psychedelic (remember that word?) song. We all four got a bang out of the public's musings on the subject and let them think whatever they wanted.

It took "Flowers" six months after its release to reach the charts. A song

131

is usually dead if it hasn't shown signs of hitting by the second or third week but due to the perseverance of a good and loyal friend, Gene Ferguson, who was also the national promotion man at Columbia Records at the time, it got more than one chance and on that final turn, radio in the Midwest finally picked it up and it gave us our first hit.

Flowers On The Wall

I keep hearin' you're concerned about my happiness
But all that thought you're givin' me is conscience I guess
If I were walkin' in your shoes I wouldn't worry none
While you and your friends are worryin' about me I'm havin' lots of fun

Countin' flowers on the wall; that don't bother me at all
Playin' solitaire till dawn with a deck of fifty-one
Smokin' cigarettes and watchin' Captain Kangaroo
Now don't tell me I've nothing to do

Last night I dressed in tails, pretended I was on the town
As long as I can dream it's hard to slow this swinger down
So please don't give a thought to me, I'm really doin' fine
You can always find me here and havin' quite a time

Countin' flowers on the wall; that don't bother me at all
Playin' solitaire till dawn with a deck of fifty-one
Smokin' cigarettes and watchin' Captain Kangaroo
Now don't tell me I've nothing to do

It's good to see you, I must go, I know I look a fright
Anyway my eyes are not accustomed to this light
And my shoes are not accustomed to this hard concrete

So I must go back to my room and make my day complete
Countin' flowers on the wall; that don't bother me at all
Playin' solitaire till dawn with a deck of fifty-one
Smokin' cigarettes and watchin' Captain Kangaroo
Now don't tell me I've nothing to do

Words and Music – Lew DeWitt

— Harold —

Holy Bible/Old Testament and *Holy Bible/New Testament* - If ever there was a group vision, this was it. We started working on this idea in the late 60s. It was simply to start at the beginning of the Old Testament and tell the major Bible stories in music. Pretty ambitious plan. We were disappointed when we were not given enough time or opportunity to record our idea at Columbia, but it turned out to be a blessing in disguise. After joining Jerry Kennedy and Mercury Records in the 70s, we were able to write and develop it the way it was supposed to be.

We literally assigned songs to each other to be written and were ever conscious to keep it scripturally correct. It was finally finished and released in 1975 as a two-album set, Old and New Testament, with twenty-two songs; we wrote fifteen of them. I think I speak for everyone when I tell you that we felt that we had done something of importance in our career. No one to our knowledge had ever attempted anything of this scale before or since. We were honored when we started to hear from ministers, Sunday School teachers and just regular folks who appreciated what we had done. We look back on it today with a lot of love. We're thankful we were allowed to tell the old, old story in our way and in our time.

— Don —

"HOW TO BE A COUNTRY STAR" - We were booked to perform on the CMA show on CBS on October 9, 1978. They wanted a song from us and it was up to us as to what it would be. Everyone sort of drifted through those shows plugging their latest single and wearing their newest clothes, so Harold and I thought we'd do something a little different. We'd write a special number tailor-made for the show. And this song would be another one short on plot but heavy on humor. A list of the things past stars have done to stand out to the public. A list of gimmicks that matched the individual country music star. An advice song, quite simply, on how to become a country star. And the last summary verse was the punch of the song.

It was an immediate hit with the industry and TV audience. We started getting calls and letters the very next day asking where the record could be bought. There *was* no record but we saw to it that there soon would be. This might be the best example in our career where a song was a hit before it was even released.

The next spring Kenny Rogers won one of the major awards at the Academy of Country Music and in his acceptance speech said, "Now maybe I'll get mentioned in a Statler Brothers song."

How To Be A Country Star

There're questions we're always hearing, everywhere we go
Like, "How do I cut a record or get on a country show?"
Well, it takes more than just ambition and three chords on an old guitar
There're a few more things you ought to learn to be a country star

You gotta learn to sing like Waylon or pick like Jerry Reed

Yodel like Jeannie Shepard or write songs like Tom T.
Put a cry in your voice like Haggard; learn Spanish like Johnny R.
Whisper like Bill Anderson and you'll be a country star

Play piano like Ronnie Milsap or Gilley or Jerry Lee
Yo-yo like Roy Acuff or talk plain like Ralph Emery
Growl like Conway Twitty; get a red, white and blue guitar
Build a swimming pool like Webb did and you'll be a country star

Be tall like Sonny James is; tell jokes like Minnie Pearl
Or be short like Jimmy Dickens; or play five-string like Earl

Get a headband like Willie's; learn to stutter like M-Mel
Get a cap like Roy Clark wore or a voice like Barbara Mandrell
Be rich like Eddy Arnold; say you're makin' more than you are
Get a gimmick like Charley Pride got and you'll be a country star

But if you have no talent and if you're not a male
If you're built somewhat like Dolly or have a face like Crystal Gayle
Come backstage and ask for Harold, Phil, Don or Lew
And we'll see you get auditioned for the Statler Brothers' Revue

Words and Music – Don Reid and Harold Reid

— Harold —

"DO YOU KNOW YOU ARE MY SUNSHINE" - It was the summer of 1977. We were playing an outdoor, Sunday afternoon, country music park in northern Indiana. It was our second show of the day and, as we would often do, we started talking and taking requests from the audience. A young lady came to the right side of the stage and motioned for me to lean over to hear her request. I did and she simply said, "Do you know 'You Are My Sunshine'?" Of course, she was asking us to sing the old Jimmie Davis song, "You Are My Sunshine." But as soon as she said it I turned it around in my head and heard it as a declaration rather than a song request. In other words, it's just another way to say 'I love you.' And that's what all songwriters are looking for; another way to say it. I couldn't wait to get on the bus to tell Don and write it down.

Now fast forward to our next recording sessions several months later. We'd been in the studio all week and needed one more song to complete our project. Don and I sat up most of the night writing the song we needed. The next morning we got up, sang it to our Brothers, arranged it and recorded it that afternoon.

After all these years we still get a letter from time to time from someone who claims to be that girl by the stage. I don't know who she was but I'd like to say thanks.

Do You Know You Are My Sunshine

She was standing in the crowd all alone and looking pretty
Listening to the music that we played
She walked up and whispered; I leaned down and listened
To the request that she made

"Do you know you are my sunshine?" she asked so sweet and tenderly
"Do you know you are my sunshine and would you do it one more time for me?"

Border to border and ocean to ocean
I still look for her every place
Chasin' the sunshine, each and every night I'm

Searchin' every crowd for her face
She was gone just as quick as the song that she asked for
Takin' my sunshine away
But someday when I finally look down and see her
I know just what I'm gonna say

"Do you know you are my sunshine? Do you know what your smile did to me?
Do you know you are my sunshine? And it looks like you're always gonna be."

Words and Music – Harold Reid and Don Reid

— Don —

"DON'T WAIT ON ME" - Sometime in 1980, George Burns decided he wanted to cut an album and Mercury, the label we were with for over 25 years, signed him. Someone, and I no longer remember who, came to Harold and me for song material for his first album. We wrote a song especially for him; one that had that backward approach to humor that he was famous for. One that... well, here's a sample verse that speaks for itself:

When the sun wakes up in the West and lays its head down in the East
When they ordain Madalyn O'Hair and she becomes a priest
When a San Diego sailor comes home with no tattoo
When the lights go on at Wrigley Field, I'll be coming home to you.

A stream of impossibilities. Things that just weren't going to happen. And one of those things that just wasn't going to happen was George recording this song. Instead of recording this one that we had worked so hard to streamline for him, he wound up cutting "Whatever Happened To

137

Randolph Scott," a song we had written and recently had a hit with and another song I wrote for no one in particular titled "Just Send Me One." We were tickled he cut two of our songs, but now we had this perfectly good and funny piece of material just lying around, not knowing what to do with it. So the next time we went in to record, which was March of '81, we put it down on tape and it was a big record for us.

But the story just kept unfolding. We performed it every night on stage and played around with the lyric and turned it into a comedy routine. And then the truly impossible happened when the Chicago Cubs announced that they were, after all these years, definitely going to put lights on Wrigley Field. They had been the one and only holdout in national sports, playing only daylight games and now they were going the way of all 'flash' and installing lights. We had gained so much attention with the song that our phones and mail were barraged with questions and comments as if we were involved in the decision ourselves. The closest we came to being involved in the controversy was being asked to come to Chicago and sing the National Anthem on August 8, 1988, the night the lights were to go on. We declined as we were home during that period and as we've explained before, summer at home when the kids were out of school was no time to ask us to add extra travel days to our schedule. And anyway, it rained that day and the lights didn't go on until the August 9.

But our most immediate question was how to handle the lyric of the song on stage. We could no longer sing "when the lights go on at Wrigley Field I'll be coming home to you." We had to alter the line and make it another impossibility, thus we did with the change, "when they put a dome on Wrigley Field, I'll be coming home to you."

We think that's safe, but who knows. They may be building one as we speak.

Don't Wait On Me

When the sun wakes up in the West and lays its head down in the East
When they ordain Madalyn O'Hair and she becomes a priest
When a San Diego sailor comes home with no tattoo
When the lights go on at Wrigley Field, I'll be comin' home to you

When the winds don't blow in Chicago and L.A. is cold and clear
When they unfurl Old Glory and no one stands to cheer
When my brother-in-law phones me and the charges aren't reversed
When the cabbie don't want a bigger tip, I'll be slidin' home from first

Don't wait on me (little darlin') Lord, can't you see (little darlin')
I only go (so far then) no guarantee
Don't wait on me (to win you) That's something I (just can't do)
Never have and don't (intend to) don't wait on me

When you load up on a long shot and he wins by half a nose
When the Fourth of July parade is called because of snow
When the waiting room is empty and the doc says, "Come right in"
When Christmas comes before New Year's, I'll be comin' home again.

Words and Music – Don Reid and Harold Reid

— Harold —

"WHATEVER HAPPENED TO RANDOLPH SCOTT" - The title pretty much sums up what was on my mind when Don asked if I had a song idea. We jumped on an old familiar subject. It gave us the opportunity to relive the Saturday mornings of our youth while making a comment on today's movies. It caught on quick and pretty soon the radio play was everything we'd hoped for. Sometimes even we forget that everybody listens to the radio.

We were on tour in southern California when the phone rang in our Hollywood hotel room and we were invited by *Mrs.* Randolph Scott to come to the office that afternoon to visit with *Mr.* Randolph Scott. He was completely retired from show business and never made appearances or granted interviews. In fact, just that week, because of the popularity of our song, he had declined appearances on two network talk shows. Mrs. Scott explained that she had waited until her family had gathered for Christmas to play our record that honored her husband. He loved it, so we went to Beverly Hills and spent the afternoon with our hero. We talked about our song. We talked about his movies and even got around to his favorite leading lady. He was a true Virginia gentleman. From the time we walked into his office till we floated out, we were all ten years old again. His favorite leading lady? Well, I can't betray his confidence, but I can't keep you from watching for a 1936 classic he starred in titled *High, Wide and Handsome*.

Whatever Happened to Randolph Scott

Everybody knows when you go to the show, you can't take the kids along
You gotta read the paper and know the code of G, PG, and R and X
And you've gotta know what the movie's about before you even go
Tex Ritter's gone and Disney's dead and the screen is filled with sex

Whatever happened to Randolph Scott ridin' the trail alone
Whatever happened to Gene and Tex and Roy and Rex, the Durango Kid
O whatever happened to Randolph Scott, his horse plain as could be

Whatever happened to Randolph Scott has happened to the best of me

Everybody's tryin' to make a comment about our doubts and fears
"True Grit" is the only movie I've really understood in years
You gotta take your analyst along to see if it's fit to see
Whatever happened to Randolph Scott has happened to the industry

Whatever happened to Johnny Mack Brown and Allan 'Rocky' Lane
Whatever happened to Lash LaRue, I'd love to see them again
Whatever happened to Smiley Burnette, Tim Holt and Gene Autry
Whatever happened to all of these has happened to the best of me

Whatever happened to Randolph Scott has happened to the industry

Words and Music – Harold Reid and Don Reid

— Don —

"WHEN THE YANKEES CAME HOME" - I love story songs. I love writing them and usually after hearing one you don't need to hear a backstory on how or why it was written because it's all right there in the lyric. But there was a little more to this particular album song and how it was triggered. I told this story to Hall of Famer Don Sutton years later after we got to be friends, but I don't know that I have ever told it to anyone else.

It was the fall of 1978 and the Dodgers and the Yankees were entangled in a battle for the World Series crown. The Dodgers had just arrived at the ballpark in New York and their starting pitcher, Sutton, was being interviewed for the evening's sportscast. When asked how he was going to feel pitching in this historical arena, he said, "When I was a kid, I always dreamed of pitching in Yankee Stadium. Of course, in my dreams, I was pitching for the Yankees." That statement and heartfelt honesty stuck with me all through the series knowing there was a story in there someplace and maybe a song. But I wasn't sure of it nor did I have the title until after the last game when I was again watching television and heard a news lady plug the fact that they would be covering the New York team's arrival at the airport as they landed victoriously on their way back from L.A. She said, "Film at eleven. The Yankees come home."

That sent my feet racing for pen and paper and my mind racing through fact and fiction to put together a love/baseball song. Of all the songs I've written and I honestly don't have a count (my sons, Debo and Langdon, could tell you quicker than I could), I can say with certainty that I have a special place in my heart for the story songs. This one didn't make me the most money but it makes me cry quicker than any I've ever written. And I guess that's why it's one of my favorites.

When The Yankees Came Home

Just a boy and his dreams and a girl in her teens
And a plan in the front of his mind
He said, "Some way I'm gonna play in the big leagues someday
Stick with me, just you wait and see in time"
Well, she waited a while, but no longer a child,
She got tired of chasing the wind
She left him one spring, Triple A, second string
And went home and married a friend

She learned to cook and learned to stitch, while he learned to pitch
A little bit better each year
And the two boys she raised were so full of praise

For the hero that they held so dear
And they yelled, "Come and see, Mom, here on TV
It's the last and biggest game of the year
The count is full, the score is tied, ninth inning, bottom side
He'll strike him out, just wait and see," they both cheered

And sure enough, there he stood like he always said he would
He was doing what he always wanted to do
That New York team he loved to hate was standing at the plate
And only she knew his dream was coming true
He proudly stood his ground out there on the mound
Facing the world all alone
And the family wondered why there were tears in Mama's eyes
'Cause she cried when the Yankees came home

Mama cried when the Yankees came home

Words and Music – Don Reid

— Harold —

"BED OF ROSE'S" - Before I can explain this one, I'll have to attempt to explain a lifelong friend we grew up with. He was a little older but a character of the first order. His name was Jack Young. He was raised in what I can safely call a privileged lifestyle. His family attended the same church as our families, although we sat where we could find a place and his family had their own pew; not by designation but by pure old Presbyterian squatters rights. Jack's father was a state senator and there are still stories about Sunday mornings when some stranger would unknowingly sit in Mr. Young's space and he would arrive and stand at the end of the pew and stare at the intruder till they moved out of his seat. I tell you this because none of this ostentatious attitude rubbed off on Jack. He was funny, smart, knowledgeable, but never phony. We spent lots of time with him over the years before he passed away much too young. He always said, "No matter when I die, they'll put young on my tombstone." That was Jack.

Now he grew up in a strangely arranged community where elegant brick homes like his were located just across the street from a less fortunate class of society. In fact, we don't remember it but Jack told us about a period of time in his life when there was a house of ill repute just across the road. He would get eggs from his mother's refrigerator and take them over to one of the 'ladies of the evening' and she would fix breakfast for this nine-year-old boy. Of course we would ask him why his parents ever allowed such a thing and he would laugh and say they had no idea. Oh, by the way, I forgot to tell you that Jack would answer almost every question with his trademark query, "Do you want the truth or a good story?" All I can tell you is we've talked to other people who knew about the late night activities of that neighborhood.

So we'd laughed for years about the story, when one day someone said to me that they considered our life and singing career to be a bed of roses, meaning, of course, soft and cushy. But my mind went back to Jack's old neighborhood and I heard the comment as a reference to 'Rose's bed.' I carried the idea around for a couple of months, never completely off my mind, but never quite coming together either. Then, of all times, I came home from church one Sunday, sat down at the piano, and wrote the entire song in fifteen minutes. That's all there is to it. Jack's story. My song. Our Rose. What did you want, the truth or a good story?

Bed Of Rose's

She was called a scarlet woman by the people
Who would go to church but left me in the street
With no parents of my own, I never had a home
But an eighteen year old boy has got to eat
She found me outside one Sunday morning
Beggin' money from a man I didn't know
She took me in and wiped away my childhood
A woman of the streets this lady Rose

This bed of Rose's that I lay on, where I was taught to be a man
This bed of Rose's where I'm livin' is the only kind of life I understand

She was a handsome woman, just thirty-five
Who was spoken to in town by very few
She managed a late-evening business
Like most of the town wished they could do
And I learned all the things that a man should know
From a woman, not approved of, I suppose
But she died knowing that I really loved her
Off life's bramble bush I picked a rose

Words and Music – Harold Reid

— Don —

"THE BLACKWOOD BROTHERS BY THE STATLER BROTHERS" -
A most unusual title and a most unusual song. I wrote this as a tribute to

some of our early heroes in gospel music who had taught us to sing and perform by example. We studied their records and stage presence and learned from the best without them ever knowing what an impact they had on our career. The song sets up a little history of our admiration, even chides them gently about all the merchandise sales and then goes into a couple of choruses of the song titles to all of their big hits in the gospel field. This song was very personal to me and each of us as we sang it but even more so as we began to know James Blackwood better through the years. And it was many years later that James' friend and biographer, Allen Dennis, a history professor at Troy University in Alabama, told me a story that touched me even more than the song. Allen, who has become a close friend of mine in recent years, says James used to like to pull out our album and play this cut and would smile all the way through it. He said to Allen one night, "If the Statler Brothers had ever decided to come fully into the gospel field, they would have been the best gospel quartet ever in the business." Then he paused and smiled again and said, "Well, maybe the second best."

That's okay, James. We loved you and we would have gladly taken a backseat as second best to the original Blackwood Brothers any day of the week.

The Blackwood Brothers By The Statlers Brothers

We all four grew up together in a small Virginia, country town
And for some strange reason, God only knows, we got to singing around
And about twice a year at the National Guard Armory or the old schoolhouse
  we'd go see
The Blackwood Brothers who were coming to town to sing especially for me

They always drew a crowd of young folk and old women and men with a
   mortgage on their home
Farmers and teachers, rich men and preachers; the old schoolhouse was full
   when they would come
And we bought up every album, every picture, every single; their autographs
   were the only things free
But the main thing they were selling was Jesus and good singing in that old
   schoolhouse where the Blackwoods sang for me

And they would sing… And they would sing
Hide Me, O Blessed Rock of Ages; Everyday Will be Sunday Bye and Bye;
Heavenly Love; Inside the Gate; Give the World a Smile Each Day;
They were all Peace Like a River to my soul

And I Wanna Cross Ol' Chilly Jordan; and I Want to be More, More Like Jesus
   Every Day
Rock-A-My-Soul in the Bosom of Abraham; At the Old Country Church;
God Made a Way for me; That's What the Good Book Says.

How Many Times, have you heard them sing these songs?
So many times, they've been our idols for so long
And God, if there's an old schoolhouse in heaven, let me be
Somewhere close where I can hear R.W. sing for me:

The Robe, The Robe, The Robe of Calvary,
And God, if there's an old schoolhouse in heaven, let me be
Somewhere close where I can hear the Blackwoods sing for me.

Words and Music – Don Reid

— Harold —

"ALL AMERICAN GIRL" - Let me say right here that you not only don't know where your next idea will come from, you also don't know how long it will take to commit it to paper. Some run like water going downhill but others are uphill all the way.

This one began in Hawaii in 1972. Don and I were walking Waikiki Beach one afternoon and were browsing a gift shop. Don reached up on the wall and took down a small guitar and quickly pulled it in tune. With no one else close by, we exchanged a song idea. Fact is, we wrote the whole first verse. We borrowed a piece of scrap paper from the clerk, wrote it down and left. No, we didn't buy the guitar. Five years later in some long-forgotten hotel room, we finished it.

Five years in the making, it's either the shortest long song in the world or the longest short song. Like I said, they're all different.

All American Girl

She's got a Texas smile you can see for a mile and a Georgia tan
A dimple in her chin and soft brown skin like Florida sand
She's got an L.A. walk, a Mississippi talk and a Boston grace
And Indiana, apple pie, hope I die mother lovin' face

But she's got an Idaho chill, a Missouri will when she gets mad
She gets wilder then than a Kansas wind when she breaks bad
Then she gets calm as a pine in North Caroline after a storm
And like the Arizona sun, we have more fun when she gets warm

She watches her stories on TV every day

And eats at McDonald's once a week to get away
She dreams of finding romance and traveling 'round the world
She's a sugar and spice, everything nice, All American Girl

She always sings along with her favorite song on the radio
She's never dressed when all the rest are ready to go
And she likes changin' her hair, something new to wear and playin' coy
But she likes it most lyin' close to her All American Boy
She roots for the loser on the Game of the Week
And loves holdin' other people's babies 'cause they're sweet
She lays in the sun and never swims so she won't lose her curl
She's a sugar and spice, everything nice, All American Girl

She's yours, she's mine, she's one-of-a-kind, All American Girl

Words and Music – Don Reid and Harold Reid

— Don —

"SILVER MEDALS AND SWEET MEMORIES" - Our bus driver, Dale Harman, lost his stepfather in 1976 who had been like a real father to him all his life. He had been in World War II and at his graveside funeral, I watched and listened as they played taps, performed the 21-gun salute and then ceremoniously folded the flag three-cornered and presented it to his widow. Before I ever got back in my car, my mind was racing with a song idea about a soldier who had died in battle and never saw the son that was born fatherless back home in the States. It was all inspired by the service I had just witnessed even though it was fictitious. Months later we recorded it and it was a hit for a generation who still remembered some WWII vets in their past. Again, the best part of the song came after the fact. One morning Dale came into my office with a package. He handed it to me and said it was from his mother and she wanted me to have it. I opened it and it was that beautiful flag, still folded in the military way. I was stunned. I told him there was no way I could accept this and he quite frankly said, "You don't tell my mother no about anything. If she wants you to have it, you're gonna have it." And I have it. I placed it on the top shelf of my office and it is there to this day. I'm looking at it right now as I write this. Top o' the morning to you, Sarge.

Silver Medals and Sweet Memories

Just a picture on a table, just some letters Mama saved
And a costume brooch from England, on the back it has engraved,
"To Eileen, I love you, London 1943"
And she never heard from him again and he never heard of me

And the war still ain't over for Mama,
Every night in her dreams she still sees
The young face of someone who left her
Silver Medals and Sweet Memories

In Mama's bedroom closet, to this day on her top shelf
There's a flag folded three-cornered, laying all by itself
And the Sergeant would surely be honored to know how pretty she still is
And that after all these lonely years, his Eileen's still his

And the war still ain't over for Mama,
Every night in her dreams she still sees
The young face of someone who left her
Silver Medals and Sweet Memories

Words and Music – Don Reid

— Harold —

"ELIZABETH" - A Jimmy Fortune special. He would take the slightest clue or inspiration and come back in a very short while with a song. This one started late one night on the bus. We put one of our all-time favorite movies in to watch and show to Jimmy. Now here's where inspiration kicks in. Phil and Don and I had seen *Giant* about 20 times. Of course, it stars Elizabeth. What do you mean Elizabeth who? Is there another one? Anyway, we're enjoying the movie and thinking we're educating Jimmy to the classics when he leaves and goes to the back of the bus and writes "Elizabeth." It was a number one record for us. A few years later, Miss/Ms./Mrs. (?) Taylor was gracious and pleased when we sang it to her. She loved it. She smiled while we sang. Now buddy, that's inspiration!

Elizabeth

O Elizabeth, I long to see your pretty face
I long to touch your lips, I long to feel your warm embrace
Don't know if I could ever live my life without you
O Elizabeth, I'm sure missing you

I remember when we shared a life together
You gave me strength and love and life that felt brand new
But you're so far away I have to say I'm feelin' blue
O Elizabeth, I'm sure missing you

O Elizabeth, I long to see your pretty face
I long to touch your lips, I long to feel your warm embrace
Don't know if I could ever live my life without you

O Elizabeth, I'm sure missing you
Well, it's been said before that I've caused many heartaches
And I wonder if that part's really true
Be it right or wrong, it feels my heart will surely break
O Elizabeth, I hope you understand

Words and Music – Jimmy Fortune

— Don —

"GUILTY" - I don't remember as much about the writing of this song as I do the subsequent arranging and recording. Harold and I usually wrote together with a guitar in my hands and a pad and pencil in his. My files and notes tell me that we started this song in Nashville in June of '82 and finished it three months later in Los Angeles. This was not an unusual pattern for us. It was also not unusual for us to write more than we needed and edit out verses and choruses before recording it. (I'll include a verse we never used for the single or the video.)

And then it was into the studio with it, but the session didn't feel right. Sometimes it's difficult to know what is wrong with a creative piece, but we felt it was the instruments or our singing or the tempo or something even more subtle. Two months after the initial recording we sent our drummer in to see if that would help with the feel of it all. It didn't, so after another month we all went back in and started from scratch. And this time we liked what we heard except for the ending and we struggled along with our producer and friend, Jerry Kennedy, to find the right one. We tried fading it. We tried the big chord on the tag. We tried just stopping. Nothing was working. And then at one point we looked up and saw we had a visitor in the studio with us. It was our old pal Conway Twitty. Here is a guy we had done shows with, shared dressing rooms with and spent countless hours just talking about life in general. A good and gracious man. I can remember looking out in the audience one Sunday afternoon during a concert in Kentucky and seeing Conway standing in the back along the wall just clapping and laughing along with everybody there. The odd thing was that he was not on the show. He was on his way home with his band from a Saturday night date and saw the marquee and just stopped and came to the show. This was the kind of unexpected thing you could always expect from Conway.

Anyhow, back to the "Guilty" session—he was recording just down the hall and came up to see what we were doing. He listened to our predicament and we discussed it and finally he said, "Would you mind a suggestion from someone who cares?" I'll never forget the way he posed that question. Nothing pushy; just sincere. We gladly welcomed his input and it is Conway's ending you hear on that record where we keep repeating and answering the same line over and over. It was magical—just like him. I speak for all of us when I tell you we miss him as much today as ever. We sang at his funeral.

Guilty

If she's changed I'll take the blame, if somehow she's not the same
If there's a distant look in her eye and she's lost the will to try
If she seems bitter of other days, seems to have lost her Baptist ways
If the truth comes harder than a lie, if she's guilty, so am I

If she's guilty, so am I, If she's forgotten how to cry
If she gets lonely and don't know why, if she's guilty, so am I

(verse never recorded)
If she comes and talks to you, and asks you what she should do
Give her hope and give her help and ask her not to blame herself
She was right more than wrong, we weren't weak; we just weren't strong
So just hold her hand and let her cry, and if she's guilty, so am I

Words and Music – Don Reid and Harold Reid

153

— Harold —

"THE LAST GOODBYE" - I'm sure you know by now that all the Brothers were songwriters except Phil. He never really tried, but I believe he would have done okay. Here's an example. We were working on our first album for Mercury. That means it was the early years and it also means that Harold, Phil, Lew, and Don were sharing a hotel room. We created a little game one night to help complete our *Bed of Rose's* album. Each of us, including Phil, would write one line secretly and see if we could get a song started.

Listen, I know what you're thinking and I'm here to tell you you'll do lots of silly stuff to pass the time on the road. We had to start somewhere so we all wrote a line. You guessed it; Phil won. His was the opening line of the song: *Afraid her tears might move my mind*. That's pretty darn good for a guy who doesn't write songs.

For all of you who are keeping score, there's only one other song written by all four of us. In 1985 we were working like crazy to finish our album *Christmas Present*. This time it was Harold, Jimmy, Phil, and Don who wrote "Mary's Sweet Smile." We were double lucky on this one because we not only felt it was a pretty good song, but we all had the Christmas spirit at the same time. We wrote it one hot summer afternoon in July.

The Last Goodbye

Afraid her tears might move my mind, I decided to drop her a line
Because where she's concerned I just ain't strong
I couldn't look her in the eye and say our last goodbye
I tried it time and time before but it went wrong

So in this letter she will find all the things that's on my mind
And I'm sure she'll find the man to do her right

I know Jim and Bill will be happy that she's free
Chances are she'll be booked up every night

And see things she'd never see, tied down to a guy like me
There's a better side of life she's never known
And I know she'll be alright once I'm gone out of her life
She may not even realize I'm gone

So I wrote it down this time and I read it line for line
But it didn't read just like I meant it to
All the things I meant to say came out sounding some other way
All the goodbyes came out sounding I love you

Words and Music – Harold Reid, Phil Balsley,
Lew DeWitt, Don Reid

Mary's Sweet Smile

Shepherds in fear of a light that shone near
Wise men from afar, followed a star
Angels did sing to the new Baby King
And the world glowed with Mary's sweet smile

Kings from the east gave gifts when they came
An angel of God gave Jesus his name
That night cast a spell that the ages will tell
As the world glowed with Mary's sweet smile

Love finds its place in a world full of grace
Men lost in sin, start new again

Still thankful, we sing to the Baby, our King
As the world glows with Mary's sweet smile

Words and Music – Harold Reid, Phil Balsley,
Jimmy Fortune, Don Reid

— Don —

"MR. AUTRY" - We have known Gene Autry's name as long as we've known our own. He's been a part of our lives as long as we've been a part of one another's. When he wrote his autobiography, we carried it on the bus with us and read it and marveled at the man he was both on and off the screen. A cowboy; a soldier; a performer; a writer; a business man; the only person with *five* stars on the sidewalk in Hollywood. Harold and I put the song together as soon as we finished the book and it was a tribute we both cherished. I remember when we first sang it on the bus to Phil and Lew, Lew cried.

There's more to tell about Gene, and we will later, but the song was never more special than when we sang it for him. We heard that he watched our TV show every Saturday night, so we did a special dedication to him, knowing he would be watching and listening. What a switch. Gene Autry watching *us* on the screen. Sometimes things like that are just more than the heart can handle.

Mr. Autry

Dear Sir, we read your book, and you gave us a closer look
At the hero who helped us know right from wrong,
Ah, it's been so long

Mr. A., we read each page, and even you improved with age
You're still the cowboy that all of us boys
Thought you were

You still ride Champion in our mem'ries
A cowboy and soldier to the end
Whenever duty called you would answer
And be back in the saddle again

Mr. A., we loved each line; you gave so much in your time
From radio to picture shows, and the songs you write,
Ah, your hat's still white
Mr. Gene, it's another day and we've grown up but let us say
Just like before and even more
We want to be like you

You still ride Champion in our mem'ries
A cowboy and soldier to the end
Whenever duty called you would answer
And be back in the saddle again

And Gene, just one more thing; if the Angels don't look good this spring
Don't worry none; you're still number one
And we still love you

Words and Music – Harold Reid and Don Reid

"SUSAN WHEN SHE TRIED" – I thought it was a pretty good song when I wrote it, but after we committed it to tape, we liked it even better than we ever imagined. We liked it so much that when we went out to eat after the session, a ritual we always indulged in with Jerry Kennedy to review the day's work, we sort of came to the mutual agreement that we would put it in the can until we had a dry spell. We thought it was that good. Of course our impatience kicked in after a year and we released it. And it was not only a hit but a terrific stage song for us. Some songs that sell records die on stage and some that never get off the ground on the radio are killers with a live audience. This one proved to be both. And the story gets even better.

Our publisher, Bill Hall, phoned me one day at home in Virginia and said he had just gotten a call from Memphis about something I may be interested in. It seems Elvis was a big fan of our song and wanted to record it for his next album. As a matter of fact, he was recording that very night in Nashville and was calling to invite me to the session. I said that was wonderful but I was in Virginia and wouldn't be able to make it. Bill went on to say there may be another phone call. He said Elvis' people had a habit of asking for half of the publishing on songs he recorded. In other words they may ask me to relinquish 50% of the publishing rights which was all legal and above board but Bill was concerned because he didn't want to lose that revenue. I assured him I didn't either being as how the Statler Brothers were the publishers on it and told him I would handle it should the call come.

The call never came. Elvis recorded the song; it was on his *Today* album and all was well. He basically did our arrangement and I was glad he did. Would I have turned down the deal if confronted with it? That's kind of like asking what if the South had won the war. I guess we'll never know.

Susan When She Tried

I got over Charlotte Thompson, Goldie Johnson, Lord they done me wrong
Took it hard with Peggy Harper, she hurt me bad but not for long
There's just one I remember, makes me feel funny down inside
I'd trade 'em all for just an hour of Susan when she tried

No there's never been a woman who could make me weak inside
And give me what I needed like Susan when she tried

It gets worse in the summer when the nights are hot and long
And it's bad in December when they play those Christmas songs
So if you ask me and I don't tell you, bet your sweet bottom dollar I lied
'Cause there's never been one better than Susan when she tried

No there's never been a woman who could make me weak inside
And give me what I needed like Susan when she tried

Words and Music – Don Reid

THE ONES THAT GOT AWAY: Songs we had first but were hits by someone else.

— Harold —

"ELVIRA" - Your first question is that you think even I have confused the Statlers with the Oak Ridge Boys. Not quite. Let's go back to 1968. We were doing a TV pilot show hosted by Jerry Naylor called *Music City USA*. Dallas Frazier, a songwriter with a new song titled "Elvira" was also a guest. Let's just say Dallas wasn't having a great day, so he wanted us to sing his new song with him. We did the best we could with four minutes to learn it and arrange it. We were glad when it was over. Dallas didn't know when it was over, but I guess it didn't matter because the show never got off the ground. I hope you never see it. So, yes, we were the first to sing "Elvira." Thankfully the Oaks were the last.

— Don —

"ME AND BOBBY McGEE" – This is one of those songs that got away. Kris Kristofferson wrote this classic in his early years in Nashville. We've known Kris from the days he was working as a janitor at the old Columbia studios. Our first encounter was one night during a Johnny Cash session in the late 60s when I passed out during a take from a poisonous bite I had gotten from one of those giant Louisiana mosquitoes the night before in Shreveport. Harold went with me to the Vanderbilt hospital and Kris drove us and stayed with us until I was released somewhere in the a.m. after every medical student in metropolitan Nashville poked on me, stared at me and consulted about me. Then a year or so later when we were practically living at the Ramada Inn during the tapings of the Cash ABC-TV show, Kris was one of the many songwriters who used to come over and hang out with us after rehearsals and tapings in our hotel rooms and we'd sing songs to one another that we had written each week. Kris sang so low in volume that we would all have to get up on the bed and lean into him to hear the lyrics when his turn came up. We heard all those great early hits before anyone else. "Help Me Make It Through The Night," "For The Good Times," and the one that just set us all back on our heels, "Me And Bobby McGee." We told him we wanted it and that we would record it as soon as we could fit in some studio time. He was pleased and said it was all ours. This was on a Wednesday or Thursday night. We went home for the weekend and came back for the next week's show with plans to record what we felt was a certain hit. But Kris met us at the hotel with his head hanging. He said he hated to tell us this but he had gone to L.A. over the weekend, got a little drunk and had sung Roger Miller the song and Roger had recorded it as his next single all in the span of a couple of days. The music charts tell the rest of the story. It was a hit for Roger and we were happy for him. And to show Kris we harbored no hard feelings we did record it later as an album cut.

I think it is possibly the best country song ever written. It has it all: story, intimacy, tenderness, poetry, simplicity. As testament to my sentiments, I kept a framed copy of the sheet music on the wall of my office for years as a reminder to myself as a writer just what a country song should be. It gave me something to work toward in those early years. I vowed not to take it down until I had done something I could be equally proud of as a writer. I took it down right after "I'll Go To My Grave Loving You."

A random memory from early '71: I ran into Kris at the front desk of the King of the Road, Roger's hotel in Nashville. We were both checking in and "Bed Of Rose's" was at the top of the charts. He said, "Which one of you wrote that song?" I said, "That would be brother Harold." He said, "Tell him I'm gonna break his fingers."

A songwriter just can't ask for a better compliment than that.

— Harold —

"DADDY SANG BASS" - This was born backstage in a dressing room long since forgotten. We came off stage one night and found Carl Perkins over in the corner, guitar in lap and humming to himself. That was always a good sign with "Perk" because he could create a song faster than he could write it down. This particular night he called us over, explained his idea and we found ourselves in the middle of his creation. I remember adding the bass line pick-up that was the song title. Carl's eyes were twinkling as they always did when he was 'rockin.' The song was finished that night and everyone raved about the great idea he'd put together.

Never being bashful about searching for your next hit, we asked Carl if we could record it. He said, "of course," and everybody was happy. A few weeks go by and we were called in to record with Johnny Cash for his new single. It was "Daddy Sang Bass." So we did get to record it but it was John's record. Ah, well, you can't win them all. Again, to show there were no hard feelings, we did put it on our *O Happy Day* album later. Great song. Sorry we missed it.

"GREEN GRASS" – You say you've never heard of it? Maybe you'll recall it in a minute. This song story begins with our first encounter in the rough and tumble politics of the music industry. Oh, yes, it's even worse here than in most industries. After our first big crossover hit in '65, everyone wanted to be part of our next "Flowers On The Wall." People sent us all kinds of songs, mostly bad or at least not suited to us.

A big time, powerful publisher in Nashville who called his own shots and most other peoples' too, brought us a song he owned called "Green Grass." Now I would tell you his name right here, but I don't want him to think I remember it. Anyway, we recorded the song and our label, Columbia, seemed to be really excited about it. It was released and we were very pleased when, after only a few days, it had sold 25,000 copies. It looked like another hit. Then out of the blue we get a phone call from Columbia saying they are 'canceling' the release. This is the first and only time we have ever heard this term. We should have been suspicious when they actually called us on the phone. You see, record execs are too important to communicate with the artists who, by the way, pay for the large salaries and even larger expense accounts enjoyed by these corporate suits.

In short, they pulled the record from the market place on orders from that unnamed publisher. It seems he had also pitched the song to Jerry Lewis' son who headed a 60s group called Gary Lewis and The Playboys. So with a couple of phone calls, we were out and they were in. They had a good record and we wished them well. As for the cheesy publisher, we swore we'd never record another song connected with him. We never did.

Sometimes just sleeping good is enough revenge.

Chapter Sixteen

I've met all my heroes and shook all the hands of all I wanted to meet
— Don Reid and Harold Reid
"I've Never Lived This Long Before"

— Don —

Somewhere in time, in someplace or another, I was asked in an interview what one thing our career had afforded us that we most cherished. This was a refreshing question from the usual "Where did you get your name" and "Are all of you brothers?" It gave me pause for a second and while I savored the originality of the query and felt a song forming in my brain, I answered in all sincerity, "It's given us an opportunity to meet all our heroes." It was a moment of unbridled truth on my behalf as I usually went into every interview with my guard high and my expectations low. Most questions were stock and shallow and I could handle them over the phone while watching "Andy" on my office TV with my feet on the desk and my mind on lunch while writing a letter and signing a stack of black and white publicity photos. This is not a testament to any extraordinary talents on my behalf but a comment on the similarity of questions one gets day in and day out. So my answer was as much a surprise to me as it was to the faceless voice on the other end of the line. It revealed a truth about me and us, the Statlers, which I had never stopped to ponder. And I liked what I heard. Our career gave us a chance to meet some wonderful and interesting people we would only have read about in any other given situation. We were blessed with some memorable relationships and unforgettable meetings with some wonderful folks of our time. Here are some random memories of a few you might enjoy.

President Jimmy Carter – We were invited to the White House a couple of times during President Carter's administration. The first time was for a State Dinner. We ate with the President and all of the dignitaries and then everyone repaired to the East Room where we were the evening's entertainment. (Forgive me—I couldn't resist saying "repaired to the East Room." It sounds so haughty and formal.)

The next time we were there we were part of a large, all-star cast that was performing at Ford's Theater and we were all invited to the White House for lunch with the President before the concert that evening. It was October 2, 1979, and we were all gathered in the State Dining room, just finishing lunch, when my 'unbashful' brother stood up and dinged his table knife against his water glass and brought the room to silence. He said, "Yesterday was the chief's birthday and being as how we've got over half of Nashville here in this room, I think the least we can do is sing Happy Birthday to him." And we did. And he seemed to enjoy it. He's a good and decent and sincere man whether you like his politics or not.

— Harold —

President Jimmy Carter – We were invited to the White House on Tuesday April 8, 1980, by President Carter and his wife Rosalynn to honor the President of the Arab Republic of Egypt, Anwar Sadat. We arrived that afternoon, under considerable security, for a sound check and run-through for that night's performance. We were met at the door of the White House by President and Mrs. Carter in their jogging outfits and they very graciously took us to the room where we would appear that night. They stayed and chatted and were everything you would expect a Georgia couple to be.

It just happened they were living in Washington on Pennsylvania Avenue at the time.

We arrived again that night in full formal dress with our proud wives to a State Dinner that we'll never forget for lots of reasons. One that is very special. During our meal, someone had confided to us that, like the Statlers, Mr. Sadat was a movie fan. I found that interesting so after I finished eating, I walked over to a Secret Service agent and asked if it would be possible or appropriate to speak with Mr. Sadat. He said, "Sure, go ahead." (Remember as far as security goes this was a very long time ago.) So I walked over to where the Presidents Carter and Sadat were seated side by side. President Carter looked up, motioned me over and I squatted down between the two world figures and talked about classic Hollywood movies.

Mr. Sadat was very cordial and excitingly told me that when he was home, most nights he would run an old movie in the palace. I couldn't help but think of all the theaters named the Palace, but this took on a whole new meaning. He also said he favored Westerns. Mr. Carter agreed. So here I was sitting between two historical icons with my hands on the backs of their chairs, talking about something even I knew a little about. It was a very special moment. I'd like to write something here really clever, but sometimes corny is best. This could only happen in America and when it happens to you, you don't question it. You just cherish it.

— Don —

President George H.W. Bush (41) – We were in Washington on a mission for First Lady Nancy Reagan, which I'll tell you about later, and were taken by the Old Executive Office Building to meet with Vice President Bush. He showed us around and shared some stories and proved to be a genuine and friendly gentleman. As we were sitting in his office he told us that he had two offices in the city: this one in the Old Executive Office Building and one in the White House next door. He said when the President was in town he came to work here but when the President was out of town he always reported to the one in the White House. That way one or the other of them was always close at hand to the pulse of the administration. Pretty good setup.

Our next meeting was after he dropped the Vice from his title. Spring of '91 found us again performing at Ford's Theater. (We were there more than Lincoln and with better results.) The President and First Lady Barbara hosted a buffet dinner in the same State Dining Room before the concert. Debbie and I were standing in the Blue Room drinking in the scenery and looking out the window when she spotted Millie, the Bush's Springer Spaniel playing on the lawn. I think this thrilled her more than any sight she witnessed the whole day, being a dog lover of the highest order. When we went through the reception line and had our picture taken with the Bushes, while shaking hands and greeting them, Debbie squealed out, "I'm so excited. We just saw Millie." At which the President jumped and said, "Where?" thinking she was running loose through the rooms. No, Mr. President, that's just my wife running loose in the rooms.

Colin Powell – At the time he was *only* the Chairman of the Joint Chiefs of Staff, before becoming Secretary of State. He and his wife, Alma, arrived late at the White House party and when she spotted us she came over and said, "Does Colin know you're here?" We said no, not knowing for sure what the question meant. Was he going to have us thrown out once he found out we were there? Or maybe throw us out himself? He probably could have done either. She went on to explain, "My husband is the biggest fan the Statlers have ever had. When he used to have to drive around the country from Army base to Army base, he always kept you in the tape deck. You have no idea how many miles you have traveled with him."

And sure enough, when he saw us, he came over, all smiles, and reiterated the same story. These are the kinds of things you're never quite prepared for—finding out that people you admire also admire you. But these are the things that make it all worthwhile. Many years later, at our final concert, we got the nicest note from him congratulating us on our retirement. Come to think of it, we got a pretty nice one from George 41 also.

It's always comforting knowing there're good people in high places.

President Richard Nixon – The first president we ever met was Nixon. We went to the White House with Johnny Cash on April 17, 1970, for a performance. His mood, the mood of the nation and the mood of the audience was very up that night because Apollo 13 had made a successful splashdown just hours before the concert began. But even in his *glee*, it was hard to see a lot of joy in his face during the show. Music did not seem to reach him or his wife. They were rather solemn and serious people. He was amiable and pleasant and a couple of years later even issued an invitation to the four of us to come to a gala at his San Clemente home in California. We weren't able to, due to our already committed schedule. Turning down a Presidential invitation is not something a good American likes to do and we were bothered at the time that there was no way we could honor his request of our presence. There were other political invitations we refused throughout our career due to not wanting to endorse or embrace candidates of either party publicly. We always lived by the creed that we wanted to sell records to Republicans, Democrats and Independents alike, but we found that when we refused an invitation we never heard from the people again. So be it.

But not the case with President Nixon. A few weeks after the event that we didn't attend, he sent each of us a nice note and a set of cuff links with the Presidential seal. You can't get more gracious than that. I've worn them with every tuxedo I've had on since.

Nancy Reagan – As you may remember, she got behind a drug prevention program in the 80s called "Just Say No." She took a lot of heat for trying to simplify a complex problem with such an off-handed slogan.

But when it all boils down to it, that's the first step. Tell yourself no. We all used to be cigarette smokers and one day back in that same decade said "enough" and quit. Harold and I saw our dad, who had an alcohol problem all the years through our childhood, just say "no" one day and never had a drink for the last ten glorious years of his life. He was our hero for that and many other reasons. So we weren't some of those who derided Mrs. Reagan for her approach or her slogan. We were asked to come to Washington and learn more about her program and become spokesmen for the cause. We met with her staff at the White House, were given the gold star tour, ate lunch there and then we were given an unsolicited audience with the President in the Oval Office. Just the Statlers and the Prez sittin' around talkin'. We knew we were being primed and paid in honors for our loyalty but we were not sure what exactly was taking place.

After the meeting we were asked if we would go on ABC's *Good Morning America* and talk about the drug abuse program to a national audience. When we agreed, we were then taken for a limo ride around D.C. and were briefed by our attorney, who was also connected to the administration, as to how we were to handle all subsequent interviews. We were to stress that this was Mrs. Reagan's program and hers alone. At no time were we to mention the President or that we had met or talked to him about it. Now the reason for all of this was never clear and still isn't. It was either that they wanted the President to be disconnected to the campaign in case it backfired in any public relations way or that they wanted this to be an image-building project for the First Lady. For whatever reason, we did as we were asked and reveled in the mystery of it all as we liked both of these people very much. We even went to Los Angeles with Mrs. Reagan and performed at a star-studded dinner that hosted all of Hollywood, bringing the anti-drug message to the movie industry. Everybody you can think of from Jimmy Stewart and Johnny Carson to Liz Taylor and Frank Sinatra were there. When we hit the stage and sang our first song, every one of those old Hollywood heroes of ours got to their feet and applauded. (Did I mention we sang the National Anthem?) Anyway, we had a ball and hopefully did a little good at the same time.

President Ronald Reagan – That meeting in the Oval Office I mentioned earlier left an indelible memory on us all. There is a huge Presidential Seal on the ceiling in the center of the room. In telling us the history of the seal, President Reagan pointed out that it was first used in 1880 by Rutherford B. Hayes. In 1945, Harry Truman had it redesigned with the eagle now turning his head in the opposite direction looking at the olive branch instead of the arrows, thus signifying peace. Old bashful Harold again said, "I like it better this way, Mr. President, because now the eagle is looking to his *right*." The President smiled and said, "Wonder if Truman ever thought about that?"

— Harold —

President Ronald Reagan – These are probably the most embarrassing and the most gracious elements ever to come together in the same story. The Statlers had a mailing list at one time that involved around 150,000 names and addresses. They were divided into several categories. We published a general newsletter; we published facts and figures for the press and general media; and we had a special list of people who would receive mailings not associated with our everyday activities. We had an excellent office staff of ladies who knew what to do and when to do it and where to mail it.

As a gift one Christmas, we had a small knife/nail file/bottle opener/ screwdriver to be mailed to our press and public relations list. You know the item. It's small, chrome and inexpensive. It's known as a reminder gift. The engraving on the side is there to keep your name in front of these folks as it hopefully lies on their desk throughout the year. It's a commercial ploy used by many people, including us. So you can imagine how upset we were when our office manager, Ann Peters, came to us just before Christmas and told us the little gift knives had also been sent to the "A" list. To this day we've never found out exactly how that happened, but it did and it meant that among a lot of other folks, the President of the United States of America, Ronald Reagan, had just received a little chrome knife from the Statler Brothers for Christmas. We felt as small as a fly speck and helpless to do anything to fix it. That is the embarrassing part of the story.

Now comes the gracious part. About a month after Christmas, we received a handwritten, personal note from ... you guessed it, Ronald Reagan. He said thanks and added it always came in handy at the ranch to have a pocketknife. That says volumes about the man. He was and always will be first class with the emphasis on class. We miss you Double R. I think I speak for the world and the country. I know I speak for the Statler Brothers.

Dean Martin – The first thing to know here is we are huge fans. We started with Martin and Lewis and have loved them both all these years. I'll have to confess that it was almost thirty years before I would watch the movie *Pardners*. I was mad and I thought if I didn't see it, maybe it wasn't true about the breakup. Of course, that's silly, but it shows you how seriously silly I was. It goes without saying what a thrill it was when we were invited to do the *Dean Martin Show*. We arrived in L.A. early in the week ready to go to work. This was back in the day when television variety shows would rehearse and walk through the show for four days and then tape on the fifth. Dean did it a little differently. Everybody *else* rehearsed the four days and he showed up to tape the fifth. (No, I won't make the obvious booze joke. He was never drunk, just absent.)

We spent our days on stage with the Golddiggers (tough work) and with Dean's musical director, Lee Hale. Lee would play Dean in rehearsal and it worked well. We were practicing a number that would put Dean in the center while two Statlers came in on each side of him. We were told to take his arm, guide him just past center stage and hand him off to the Golddiggers and so on. Lee stopped us one afternoon in the middle of the number and asked Phil what harmony part he was singing. Phil told him baritone and Lee says, "Oh, no. We'll have to put Don on Dean's right side because he'll sing whatever he hears in his ear and Don is singing the melody."

And so it went. Dean showed up on show day, shuffled through the entire thing, got pushed and shoved to his marks and looked better doing it than all the rest of us put together. Any performer you can recall is remembered for their looks, their talent, or their appeal. He had all of those things plus he was Dean Martin. Enough said.

★ ★ ★ ★

We always felt blessed and confident but we didn't always feel worthy. Especially like the time we arrived a day early in Vegas for a week at the MGM Grand. We were following Dean. He closed his week one night; we opened our week the next. We were in the audience for his late show and he invited us backstage to say hello. In conversation I asked him why he never sang "Memories Are Made of This" on stage. He said, "Oh, lord, I haven't done that for twenty years." I said it had been more like thirty. He smiled and indicated to us that he hadn't even thought about it for a very long time. Several years later it occurred to us that he never sang any hits from the Martin and Lewis era. Has anyone else ever thought about that? I don't know. I don't even know if he'd thought about it.

Anyway, that night he introduced us from the stage, had us stand up and told the audience to be sure to catch our show the next night. As he was plugging our appearance, it occurred to me that our billing was the same as his, but he was such a hero to us that we'd never feel worthy. He was born in Steubenville, Ohio, just a few mountains over from our Shenandoah Valley, but planets away from the way we thought of ourselves compared to the way we thought of him. But you know what? I'm sure he felt the same way about Bing Crosby.

— Don —

Dean Martin – When Martin and Lewis split up, we went with both of them. Dean took on the TV series, which we guested on and then he called us to do a Christmas special with him on NBC. Also on the show, best I remember, was Michael Learned from *The Waltons*, Georgia Engel from the *Mary Tyler Moore Show*, Freddy Fender and The Golddiggers, the group of six girls who always hovered over Dean and danced and sang and basically prettied up the set. The rehearsals for that show are vivid, still in my mind. Much was done on the beach where we ran and danced for days with the Golddiggers. I ripped the dress off one of them on the tennis court. Now it wasn't like you might think. We were dancing past the camera, which I don't do very well at all, and I stepped on the hem of her dress and ripped the whole back out of it. If only I had stepped with the other foot I might have ripped the whole front out. But as I have already inferred, my foot control is not all that accurate.

The rest of the days were spent at the horse ranch of Greg Garrison, Dean's producer and right arm. It was about an hour outside L.A. in the mountains. We did an opening scene there where the whole cast rode bikes down a country road while singing. One snag was that Georgia Engel could not ride a bicycle. Just never learned as a kid, I suppose, so they gave her a little pony with a guide rope on it so she could sort of trot along with the rest of us and pull that pony. Well, every time we rehearsed and shot the scene and she would race to keep up with all of us on our bikes, Harold would come up beside her and say out of the corner of his mouth, "Hurry up. Let's go. You're slowing everybody down." The poor girl was completely exhausted and run ragged after about three takes. At one point, Freddy Fender was pedaling alongside me and looked over out of the corner of his eye and in his best B-Western-Mexican-Alphonso Bedoya-accent said, "Your brather's no goud."

But the Dean Martin part of this story was the fact that he was about three days late for the whole shoot. As Greg explained to us with a twinkle in his eye, "He caught a cold about 2 o'clock this morning." This meant we worked around him. We shot around him and even used a stand-in for at least one of the songs. We were on the beach down at Malibu for a night scene when Greg turned up his collar and they shot him from the back of the head while we all reacted to him and the soundtrack bleated out "Marshmallow World."

Still two more days passed, but come the fourth day with the entire cast on location by the corral, in costume at six-thirty am on a frosty California-in-the-mountains morning, Dean's limo pulls up. The back door slowly opens and Dean gets out in his jeans, western jacket and black cowboy hat, looks at all of us looking at him, rubs his chin and then says in true Dean Martin fashion, "Is Jerry here yet?"

Lord, the memories are all I need.

Jerry Lewis – This was the other object of our show business affection since childhood. But until the spring of '95, we never really crossed paths with Jerry. We did his Labor Day Telethon once, but we were in one city and he was in another, so it was all business. But in early 1995, he opened on Broadway in *Damn Yankees*. My son, Debo, who is as big a Martin and Lewis fan as Harold and I ever were, said he wanted to go up and catch the show. Ever since the kids were small, we've been going to New York a lot to shop, eat and see plays. We all still love it, so I said I'd check into it. I got in touch with Jerry and he invited all of us backstage after the performance—all of my family and all of Harold's. We visited with him and he told stories and charmed everyone with just being Jerry Lewis. A couple of months later he sent me a picture and a note for my 50th birthday. It sets in a prominent place by my chair and in my heart.

John Ritter - This one has to tie in with the Jerry Lewis story. We had known John since his teen years when Tex would bring him to the shows we played together. Then after *Three's Company* was a hit, we did a variety special together where he hosted and we sang. We kept in touch with his mother, Dorothy, who had moved to Nashville so we still bumped into one another every so often.

The night we went backstage to see Jerry in New York, John and his fiancée, Amy Yasbeck, were there with his *Hearts Afire* co-star, Markie Post, and her husband. They were there to visit with Jerry, too, so it was like old home week for all of us. After the show, after the visit, and after everyone had left the theater, we all went out the back door to our waiting limos. My family was in one car with my future daughter-in-law, Alexis, sitting beside me. Someone knocked on the side window, I rolled it down and it was John. He leaned in and said, "How much better does it get? Can you believe we were just in there hobnobbing with Jerry Lewis?"

As he left and I rolled the window back up, Alexis looked at my son, Langdon, and said, "I've got to call my sister to tell her I just met Jack Tripper."

Give 'em Jerry and all they see is Jack! I never got a chance to tell John this story but I know he would have loved it.

— Harold —

Elizabeth Taylor – I told you the story earlier about the recording of the song "Elizabeth." Fortunately for us it was a hit, so the word got around that Elizabeth Taylor had been the inspiration.

We were on tour in the Southwest when we received a phone call from a production head who was in Old Tucson filming a movie that starred Miss Taylor. It seems that each morning when she arrived on the set all production would cease while they presented her with a small gift. (If that ain't old Hollywood, I'm a blind shortstop.)

Anyway, the producer who called us suggested that after we had played our concert in Tucson, as we left town the next morning, we might stop by and present the daily gift and sing "Elizabeth" to Elizabeth. I'll be honest with you here—it's hard as hell to find something wrong with that idea. So bright and early the next morning we were ushered onto the set just seconds before our 'songsake' was to appear. They handed us a small wrapped package and when she walked in, we sang the chorus of our song and presented her the gift. To this day I still don't know what was in that little box. I don't remember the day of the week or the weather. What I do remember are those deep violet eyes. Is she as beautiful as they say? You bet!

She had been filming there for a couple of weeks but no one from the outside world had even caught a glimpse of her. There were a lot of fans outside waiting, so we were pleased when she turned to us and said she would go out and say hello and have some pictures taken if we would go with her. That's like asking a drowning man if he'd like a life raft.

The five of us went out, took pictures and talked to the people gathered there. Since that day, I've never made a joke about her many marriages. I could see then how very easy it would be to fall in love with Elizabeth.

Joan Crawford – It was a festival in Jackson, Mississippi. There were a lot of people there from the wide range of this thing called "entertainment." There were recitations by Cornelius Otis Skinner. There was comedy and song by the Statler Brothers and Tennessee Ernie Ford and there were special guests who just showed up but weren't required to do anything. One of those special guests was none other than Joan Crawford, movie queen, and I'll go on record right here to tell you we have always been fans of this magnificent MGM star.

As night fell on the Mississippi, we found ourselves at the Governor's mansion and a reception that included everyone who had participated in the three-day affair. I'll be the first to tell you that we were glad to be there but were not the most famous name in the room. It was 1968 and the fact is we were mostly known for our first hit, "Flowers On The Wall." Well, it seems there was at least one other person there who just "loved that little song to death." (His words, not mine.) He was excitable and a little flighty and I'm being kind. He was working for Joan Crawford. In fact, at the time, she was confined to a wheelchair for which he was the designated driver. He followed us around and after a while asked us to please let him introduce us to his boss-lady. We said we'd like that very much.

He went into the next room and came back pushing the chair much too fast with the diminutive Miss Crawford holding on for dear life. He said, "I want you to meet the Statler Brothers who had that little song, 'Flowers On The Wall.' So anytime you hear 'Flowers On The Wall' you'll know they're singing it just to you." At this point he pulls up in front of us and completes his enthusiastic introduction. We said "hello" and "nice to meet you" and "we're lifelong fans" and "what a pleasure for us." The only thing the young man had forgotten was that Joan had not heard the song. She was not a fan of the Brothers and probably had never heard of us. On top of that, she didn't care.

So if you've ever seen a lady shopping for a cantaloupe and finally she picks up one that is rotten, you've got the picture. Her eyes roll; her nose turns up; and she wants to get out of there as fast as she can. That was the reaction of Miss Crawford to us. She made a slight sound and I couldn't tell if it was a greeting or gas. She was not impressed. That's okay because I still think she deserved the Oscar for *Mildred Pierce*. She just acted better on the screen than she did in person.

— Don —

Frank Sinatra — It was at that Nancy Reagan All-Star Hollywood bash. At the end of the show we were to go back on stage with Burt Reynolds, Donna Summer, and Frank Sinatra. Harold and Phil were to enter stage right with Burt, and Jimmy and I were to enter stage left with Sinatra. While Donna performed, Jimmy and I found ourselves lounging in the wings with the Chairman of the Board. We had never met the man and there was no one there to properly introduce us so I took it upon myself to do the honors. But just before I took that final step, I said to myself, "What do I have to say to this man he's not already heard? What compliment is there he didn't get tired of hearing thirty years ago?" So as I walked toward him and our eyes met, I searched for and found a common denominator that would be an interesting opening to me and even to him. Since high school, my favorite author has been John O'Hara. From that I came up with a subject that offered me some information I always wanted and offered Frank Sinatra a topic no one else had probably ever approached him with.

As we shook hands I said, "I know you did *Pal Joey*, which I loved and which was written by John O'Hara. I've read everything he ever wrote but never got the opportunity to meet him. Did you know him?"

He smiled and said, "Yeah, I knew him."

I said, "Tell me something about him. Just any story or tidbit."

I could tell by the expression on his face and the gleam in his eye he was reflecting on pleasant memories and he began to tell me what I wanted to know. He told me all about O'Hara and how he was always quitting something every time he saw him. He was quitting smoking or quitting drinking or quitting eating. Always trying to make some change in his life.

He chuckled at these memories and I cherished each chuckle. We had a nice visit and never once had to resort to over-flattery or severe fawning. Say what you want, but he made me a memory I couldn't refuse.

— Harold —

John Wayne – We arrived in Nashville for a week of recording dates and found that the whole town was buzzing with the news that John Wayne was there for a few days to help promote a friend's career. That's the good news. The bad news was he wasn't seeing or meeting anyone outside of the business meetings already arranged. We were as disappointed as everyone else because after all it *was* John Wayne.

So a couple of days go by and we're deep into our album and no one has seen hide nor hair of the Duke. We get back from lunch to begin a two p.m. session when our publishing representative, Bill Hall, calls and says if we can come over to the hotel, the big cowboy is waiting to meet us. It's the only time in our career we've walked out of a studio, left the musicians sitting and the clock running. The only thing we took with us was our producer, Jerry Kennedy.

We arrived at the hotel, took the elevator up and when we got to the room, were greeted by John Wayne, the biggest movie star in history. There he stood, smoking a cigar, and even in his sock feet he was still ten feet tall. We filed by him, introduced ourselves and visited for a while. Like kids in a candy store we wanted to talk about movies. He told us a great story about his early career.

He was assigned, as a very young actor, a series of Westerns called *Singing Sandy*. They wanted to make him a singing cowboy. He said he couldn't sing and he couldn't play the guitar. So they put him on a horse and to his right, off camera, was a singer. To his left, off camera, was a guitar player. He said it was very awkward and uncomfortable, so he went to Herbert J. Yates, who owned the studio, and said, "Yates, you need to go out and hire yourself the best damn cowboy singer in the world. And he did. He hired Gene Autry."

Great story; great afternoon; and a great memory. That evening after our recording was through, Jerry Kennedy said he may not be back the next morning and when we asked why, he explained. It seems that Wayne was a little hard of hearing in one ear so when Jerry introduced himself, John thought he said Duffy instead of Jerry. In fact he had said, "Nice to meet you, Duffy." Jerry said first off you don't correct John Wayne and secondly he was flying home to Shreveport, going to the courthouse and have his name officially changed to Duffy. He said, "If it's okay with John Wayne, it's okay with me."

Bill Hall arranged the meeting. We never found out how, but we're grateful to him for a memory that's bigger than life. And so was John Wayne.

Mae West – It was late November 1975 and we were in Hollywood for some television appearances. The timing was terrific because we'd just finished a road tour and the wives were flying to California to meet us and go Christmas shopping. We did all the things that mean more when the girls are there. We went to dinner high above Hollywood at the Magic Castle. It's an old mansion devoted to the ancient art of deception. There's a piano that takes requests, talks back to you, then plays your song all by itself. No piano player. You're free to go from room to room to watch close-up magic and card tricks and standing two feet away you still don't know how they did it. We went to Beverly Hills to shop and cruised the Sunset Strip. Yes, you can be an artist, a fan, and a tourist at the same time. Mike, our public relations guy, called us one afternoon and asked if we'd like to meet Mae West. We asked, "When?" He said, "Tonight." We asked, "Where?" He said, "Her apartment."

Now folks, that puts a whole new meaning to "Why doncha come up and see me sometime?"

Then Mike explained the ground rules. We were to arrive at her building at 9:30 p.m. We did. There was a gentleman who took us through the lobby and up on the elevator. We were then ushered into her retro 1930s apartment. It was decorated entirely in white. The carpet, the drapes, even the piano was white. A female assistant appeared out of nowhere and welcomed us and invited us to have a seat. We did. We waited and waited and started to wonder if someone was playing a joke on these hillbilly movie fans. A few more minutes passed and the assistant appeared again and said, "Miss West will be out in a few minutes."

We were looking around, trying to remember how to get out of there, when suddenly the curtains parted in a doorway and "da-da," Miss Mae West. She was dressed in a white gown, full makeup and every hair, supposedly, in the right place. Now we thought we were *in* a movie. All I could think of was how small she was. Really small. Maybe five feet tall. Maybe five-five counting the wig. She was cordial, gracious, but obviously on stage.

This is the first time I've ever tried to put it into words. Okay, here's a word for you. Bizarre! Please don't get me wrong. I'm not making fun. It was thrilling, interesting, curious and sad all at the same time. But after all it was Mae West and we *did* get to go up and see her one time.

— Don —

Oprah Winfrey – The name of this sub-chapter could be "The Day I Nearly Killed Oprah."

Scene One – A celebrity charity softball game. The team rosters were a sight to see. Harold and Jimmy covered the outfield on their team with Roger Miller while other positions were attended to in different stages of efficiency by Betty White, Barbara Mandrell, Dick Clark, L.L. Cool J, Chuck Norris, Erma Bombeck and Walter Payton. Didn't I say it was a sight? There were others; I just can't recall them all right now.

Phil and I shared a team with Bob Hope, Meat Loaf, Sheena Easton, Lynn Swann, John Stamos, Herschel Walker, Minnie Pearl and Oprah herself. And there were others here, too. But do you really need more?

Bob Costas and Paul Shaffer were the on-the-air broadcasters and ESPN taped the whole event, but I don't remember ever seeing it played. But I do remember getting a pretty good hit and rounding the bases only to have Walter Payton reach out at shortstop and pick me up by one arm and hold me there in the air until someone threw him the ball and he tagged me out. It was that kind of game.

But back to Madam Oprah. I was in center field and she was playing second base. Chuck Norris was up and after a long dry spell in the outfield, I was looking forward to a little action. (Betty White and Dick Clark weren't exactly power hitters.) But here came Chuck and he slammed one to center field and I ran over and grabbed it on the first bounce. Now in the excitement of things, as I was coming up with the ball, I forgot momentarily that I was on a mixed-celebrity team, so I came up throwing. And who was standing there in the line of fire behind second base in proper cut-off position but Lady Winfrey in all of her glory. I fired it straight at her and realized just as it left my hand what I had done—but too late now. She stood her ground for as long as she could but finally, at the last second, bailed out, running with her hands over her head. I came just that close to changing television history forever. Another inch to the left and Phil Donahue might still be the queen of daytime TV as we speak.

— Harold —

Marty Robbins – Marty was a funny, talented, and strange man. Let me explain. We've been fans since the fifties when he musically wore "A White Sport Coat and a Pink Carnation." Years later we toured with him on occasion and became friends. We've spent many hours sitting in dingy dressing rooms and sharing news, gossip and solving the world's problems. It wasn't unusual to glance over while on stage and see Marty making faces or motions to distract you. We've certainly done the same to him. We guested on Marty's syndicated TV show and had a blast. Because we did more laughing than singing, we enjoyed his company and believed it was mutual.

We were hosting the *Music City News Awards* show on TV in June of 1981. We introduced Marty, who ironically sang "A White Sport Coat and a Pink Carnation," and he came on to a great ovation. As we had done many times before, we attempted to have fun with an old friend, so Lew and I started dancing cheek-to-cheek on the side of the stage. Marty looked over, smiled and went on with his song. We went backstage and thought no more about it until the following day when our agent, Dick Blake, told us he had heard Marty was upset. I tried several times that week to find him but he was on tour. I finally spoke to him late one afternoon on the phone in his hotel room. I told him I had called to apologize. He promised me he understood and knew we never meant to belittle him in any way. He said everything was okay.

Now fast forward to June 7, 1982. We were again hosting the *Music City News Awards* show. Now remember that any live television show requires the audience to be in their seats at least five minutes before air time. We were introduced and sang our opening song, but when we started our opening dialogue to introduce the show, Marty made an entrance that consisted of walking the entire width of the Opry House while waving to fans and stopping to shake hands with everybody along the way.

I never talked to him again because he died the following December. All I have is his word that everything was okay.

— Don —

Roy Acuff – Our paths crossed so many times with Roy through the years. Early in our career, just as we were beginning to headline our own stage shows, Roy was working with us one night. Knowing how successful he had been for decades and that he owned the other half of Nashville that Eddy Arnold didn't, we were a little baffled at why he was even out there on the road at his age and stage in the game. He explained, "I just work enough to give the boys in my band a little income."

(It was many years later before we understood exactly what he was saying. We would have retired a few years before we did if it hadn't been for putting so many of our people out of work—our band, our bus drivers, our road crew, our office staff. We tried every way in the book to work just a couple of days a month and make it work for them, but it just wasn't possible to do. You have to either be *in* the business or be *out* of it.)

We were doing *Hee Haw* one evening when Roy sang a gospel song he had written called "The Man I'm Looking For." We flipped over it and I told him we wanted the lyrics to it. He promised he would get them to us. Well, the next time we saw him was about a month later when we were guests on a network TV special on stage at Opryland. Roy was too, and there was a finale where we were all lined up for the cast song. We were right in the middle of a dress rehearsal when Roy looked at us and remembered he had those lyrics we wanted. He also had his own dressing room at Opryland with just his things in it. His pictures on the wall, his piano, his private bath. So smack in the middle of running this song on camera with full cast and orchestra, Roy leaves the stage and comes back out and walks up to me and hands me the lyric sheet and begins telling me about how he wrote the song. Rehearsal comes to a screeching halt. The music quits playing; all the other acts turn and listen, and the director comes out of his booth and stands and stares at us. We must have held up production for a long five minutes. I felt conspicuous and on the spot but he never paid any attention to it at all. I guess we both had these different feelings because he was Roy Acuff and I wasn't.

In Roy's final years, when he was a widower and living all by himself, he had his home on the grounds at Opryland. His front door was just a few steps from the backstage entrance to the Opry House. When we were doing our TV series, we would always have an evening meal catered at six o'clock for the cast and crew. Every evening you could look down the hall at 5:45, just before we broke for dinner, and see Roy come in the side door, get himself a plate and go around the table and then quietly out the door again, taking his supper home to eat alone.

— Harold —

Minnie Pearl – You may laugh at Minnie Pearl, but no one laughed about her. She was a consummate professional. Don't let the funny hat and the mountain accent fool you. She knew what she was doing and always put considerable thought and work into her art.

We were on a large package show in coastal Mississippi one night with Minnie. She was paying us the considerable compliment of how she appreciated our comedy, our timing and material. I thanked her and added that what I hated most was breaking in new stuff. She said she totally understood and then added something I've never forgotten. She said you should never hit the stage with all new jokes. Always take a few old routines you can depend on and work in the new ones till you're comfortable. Great advice! We always practiced that and it always worked. It proved to be as dependable as Minnie herself.

Hurricane Hugo – We were on tour in September 1989 when Hugo was threatening the southern United States. It hit just north of Charleston, South Carolina, on September 22 as a category four hurricane. We rushed from one TV set to the next and watched and prayed that the wind and rain would turn northeast and not go on the west side of the mountains to our homes in the Shenandoah Valley. It turned. We were spared, but as we were giving thanks, we realized that it had done a lot of damage to people and places not as fortunate as us. That's when we decided to organize a benefit concert for the affected areas.

We were forced to hold the event in Jacksonville, Florida, because all the auditoriums and arenas in South Carolina had been damaged. We worked with Governor Carroll Campbell and the South Carolina Governor's office and were able to pull together the All-Star Benefit Concert by December 13, 1989. We headed it up but with some great folks who gave their time and talent. The ABC (All-Star Benefit Concert) was emceed by Ralph Emery and starred George Jones, the Judds, Ronnie Milsap, Ricky Skaggs, Barbara Mandrell and the Statler Brothers. We raised lots of money and it was a huge success, but there was one embarrassing moment. We were in a hurry to put it all together, so I sat down one day and sketched a design to put on a commemorative tee shirt. The company said they thought my concept was good so they went ahead with thousands of shirts. There was only one problem. Not thinking this was to be used, I overlooked the fact that I had misspelled Ricky Skaggs' name (Scaggs). Of course, I apologized but Ricky laughed and said he'd rather leave it that way because then I would owe him one. He's a great guy and it proves once again things like this could never be done in any other competitive industry. When you get past agents, managers, and secretaries, you've got people, and truth is, we're not all that different.

— Don —

Kurt Vonnegut – Could there be a stranger coupling than Kurt Vonnegut and The Statler Brothers? Even he found it unusual. He and his then wife, Jill, would come to our shows when we were in upstate New York. They were true fans. They'd come backstage and get their pictures taken with us and would really lose themselves in the music. He wrote about us in his

1981 book, *Palm Sunday*, and what he said was typical Vonnegut prose. He called us "America's Poets" and said he would like to see our song, "Class of '57," become the National Anthem. That as Olympic winners stood with medals around their necks, he would like to hear Americans sing, "Where Mavis fin'ly wound up is anybody's bet," with tears streaming down their cheeks. I don't even know what that means. But he printed out every lyric of the song in his book and seemed very sincere about it.

Jill threw him a big sixtieth birthday party with all of his writer and show biz friends and wanted us to come to New York to surprise him. We couldn't, so she asked if we would call at exactly 7:00 p.m. EST and sing "Happy Birthday" to him as he entered the ballroom. We agreed and on the day of his party found ourselves out West looking for a phone at 4 o'clock PST. This was before cell phones, so here we were rambling through the California desert searching for a pay phone and then standing by the road with traffic zipping by us singing "Happy Birthday, Dear Kurt, Happy Birthday to you."

Johnny Cash – There's time for one final Johnny Cash story. The last one. I sleep with the radio on and I had just woken up about 5 a.m., September 12, 2003, and still in a fog and turning over to go back to sleep, heard the news report that Johnny Cash and John Ritter were dead. I seriously thought it was a bad dream and it kept me awake till the next headlines at five-thirty. Then I knew that both of these unrelated stories were true. And to be honest, I was more shocked over John Ritter's death than I was over Johnny Cash's. John Ritter was three years younger than me so I had never associated death with him but Johnny Cash had just lost June four months earlier and we had been expecting the call any day. It came too soon for us, but not for him. He was rearing to go.

I lay there in bed, knowing the phone would start ringing any minute, and reminisced in my mind and turned over memories I hadn't visited for years. The beginnings; the fun; the unsure, and always sure way he grabbed life by the back of the neck. We have been asked so many times about it since the movie came out, and to set the history lesson straight, yes, we were there at Folsom and on the stage that night in Canada when he proposed to June. We were with him at his best and at his worst. And we knew we should be with him for this.

Phil, Harold and his son, Wil, and my sons Debo and Langdon, and I took off for Nashville the next day. We saw and hugged old friends at the funeral home and even more at the funeral; his daughters whom we had known since they were little girls and his son whom we had known since birth. And watching the parade of memories dance through my mind, I was comforted, as I sat there, by something comforting John had done for me so many, many years ago.

Our dad passed away in the summer of '67 and we took Mom with us to a couple of cities we were playing close by a few weeks later just to get her away. We put her on the front row and she seemed to be having a good time. We did our part of the show and John had gone out and was performing his portion, when a stagehand came back and got Harold and me and said, "Thought you might want to know, your mother is crying." We rushed to the side of the stage only to find John singing to her. He was singing the old Stuart Hamblen song, "These Things Shall Pass."

These things shall pass and some great morning
We'll look back and smile at heartaches we have known
So don't forget when storm clouds gather
The Lord our God is still the King upon His Throne

Whatever you've heard or read about him, don't believe all of it. He was a good man.

— Harold —

Roy Rogers – Everyone has heroes and there is nothing more satisfying than finding your heroes to be all you wanted them to be and even more. That's the perfect description for Roy Rogers. I have loved his good-guy image my entire life. When I was very young, my Aunt Ethel used to tell me if she heard any more about Roy Rogers from me she was going to put me in a box and mail me to him. Even then I didn't see that as a threat. It seemed to me it just might work.

We had met Roy several times and he had guested on one of our TV specials, so in the summer of 1988 when I was traveling across the country on vacation with my entire family, it was the perfect idea to stop in Victorville, California, for them to meet one of my favorite people. Victorville was where Roy and Dale lived and maintained a large museum. Roy had been contacted and had promised to meet us there early on a Monday morning. When we arrived he greeted us from an upstairs porch and told us to come on up.

He took us to his office and introduced us to his old dog that would howl when Roy yodeled. He walked us through every corner of the building. He told us stories about the displays. He explained every item in detail and when we stopped in front of a mounted and rearing Trigger, he got tears in his eyes. And so did I.

He did all this for me and my family and I'll never forget that. It has been said that you can tell the character of a man by the way he treats someone who can do nothing for him. That sums up my hero. I'll always be a little buckaroo from Virginia and he'll always be the King of the Cowboys.

★ ★ ★ ★

We were standing backstage during rehearsal for one of our TV specials chatting with Roy and he was telling stories. I think the one he told about

Gabby Hayes is my favorite. He said there was no one in Hollywood who was a more immaculate dresser than Gabby. He would arrive at the studio in a three-piece suit and tie and never go into his Gabby character until he'd slip into his patched pants and flop hat. He had pet names for Roy and Dale— Peckerwood and Satchelass—respectively. Roy confessed that he saw Gabby as a father figure and loved him very much.

The story goes that they had finished a film one spring and were free for about three months. When they got together in late summer, Roy commented to Gabby that he hadn't seen him in all that time. Gabby said, "Yeah, Roy, I did a really stupid thing. I shaved off my beard and you know what? I looked in the mirror and I was staring at the ugliest old s.o.b. I've ever seen in my life. So I went up in the mountains till it grew back."

I remember thinking he must have had his patched pants on then because that's pure Gabby Hayes.

— Don —

Roy Rogers – We did our first 90-minute TV special in 1981. Jim Owens, our producer, felt it was time we put on the screen what we had been putting on record. So we started writing the script and planning the guests. We were never shy when it came to asking people to be on our shows. We started with the best and always seemed to get them. And who could be a more obvious choice than our boyhood hero, Roy Rogers?

We had met Roy, worked with him a couple of times, the first being back in 1969 in Old Tucson for a Western special. We all wound up on a soundstage, recording the soundtracks one night. And we had a memory we just couldn't shake. Roy and Dale were standing beside us and when it came time for their duet, Roy had a little trouble with the harmony, as everyone does from time to time (except maybe Phil), and Dale jumped his case right in front of us and everybody. Hey, you can't do that to Roy Rogers. Don't you know who this is?

So we decided we wanted Roy to ourselves and by himself. We called and asked and he said he would do the show. We were elated. The next step was what song or songs to do with him. Thus one of my strangest moments in show business.

We were at our offices in Staunton, Virginia, working on the script. It was late afternoon and the day was winding down and everyone had gone home except our office manager, Ann Peters, and me. I heard the phone ring and in a few minutes she came to my office door and said, "There's a call you're going to want to take."

I said, "Who is it?"

"Roy Rogers."

On the phone for me. Roy Rogers. Everyone else had gone home, so I picked up the phone and heard, "Don, I've been thinking about a song we can sing together. There's an old thing called "Ride, Cowboy, Ride." I used to do it with the Sons of the Pioneers. Here's how it goes. Tell me if this is alright with you." And he began to sing the song to me over the phone. Then he yodeled a verse. And I'm sitting there holding the phone and saying to myself, "Roy Rogers is asking my permission to sing this song on our show? Does he not realize we know every word of it? That we sat through every movie he ever made and know all the names of all of the Sons of the Pioneers? And he's asking me, little Donnie Reid from the third row at the Strand, if this will be alright?"

When he finished, I managed to say, "Roy, anything you want to do is a done deal."

He said, "Great! I'll see you guys in Nashville in two weeks."

And he was gone. Like all the cowboy heroes of all my yesteryears. But two weeks later we were together and he was standing between us and we were singing and the harmony was perfect. We have one of his hats.

Gene Autry – In 1985 we began plans to do a two-hour television Christmas special. Again we weren't shy in coming up with a guest list. We got old friends Roger Miller, who kept us laughing for days until we all lost our voices; Crystal Gayle who had us as guests on her TV special and who would become an integral part of our series a few years in the future; and Merle Haggard who brought our Christmas spirit to its knees when we asked him on camera to share one of his most memorable holiday memories and he ad-libbed a story that began, "In 1956 I woke up in jail naked on Christmas Eve." Now there's a Christmas show for you. All we needed to round that baby out was Gene Autry and he said yes.

The only snag was that Gene was of an age and position in life…okay, he was too old and too rich to go anywhere he didn't want to, so he said if we brought the show to him he'd do it. The four of us flew to L.A. with Marshall Grant and our director, Steve Womack, and set up cameras in Gene's office and we sat on the sofa and he told stories. What a treat from a man who is as synonymous with Christmas music as Bing Crosby. He told us two great "stories behind the songs."

He had a recording session and got three songs down on tape with twenty minutes left; hardly time for another. But his wife, Ina, insisted he try one that she really liked and his arranger agreed they shouldn't waste the twenty minutes, so they pulled out and rushed through a little ditty called "Rudolph the Red-Nosed Reindeer"—the second biggest selling song in music history behind "White Christmas."

But the story of another standard a few years before is the one that tells the character of the cowboy of our dreams. He was the Grand Marshall in the annual Santa Claus Lane Parade in Hollywood in 1946 and as he was riding Champion down the street he saw all of the kids looking *past* him saying, "Here Comes Santa Claus." Many people in the entertainment world would have taken offense to being upstaged by an actor in a fuzzy red suit. But not Mr. A. He found the humor in it and the next day called his songwriting partner, Oakley Haldman, and turned a public lemon into Christmas pudding.

It's not often when a hero becomes a friend and he's still your hero.

— Harold —

Gene Autry – We were in sunny Los Angeles for one reason and that was to sit down with our hero to tape a segment for our Christmas special. You can't do better than Gene Autry and Rudolph when it's time for Santa. The only problem was, it wasn't time for Santa. It was September 24, 1985. Sometimes when you record or tape yuletide projects you have to catch the Christmas spirit really early. So before leaving Gene's office that morning, he invited us to go with him to see his beloved Angels play baseball. That evening we sat in his multi-room suite high above the stadium with the multi-millionaire cowboy and Pat Buttrum and Phil Harris thrown in for good measure. That was far and away more than anyone would expect from this very gracious man. But there was more to come. As we were leaving the game, Gene asked us if we could come to his house the next afternoon to visit and hear a Christmas song that he had found. We assured him there was nothing else on our schedule that would keep us from being there. I couldn't imagine what would be more important than that.

We arrived the next day and spent a golden afternoon that's hard to put into words, but I'll try. As I look back on it now, we were treated by Gene in two equal parts. One, as fellow entertainers and two, as the front row kids that we'd always been. He took us to every room of his house. He played us the Christmas song. (No, I don't remember the title but if Gene Autry says it's a good Christmas song, I'm not going to argue.) He let us look in closets at the rows of boots and suits lined up just like the long ago pictures in *Life* magazine. In his office and den there were volumes of leather bound scripts of every one of his movies and the walls were crowded with pictures and awards. He told us that he'd lived in this home since the early forties and even showed us around the grounds outside.

We had arrived earlier in the week to tape a guest shot with our hero. We left California with a new friend. It not only continued until his death but to this day we are included on guest lists and Christmas remembrances by his lovely widow, Jackie. She represents him even now with love and respect.

As boys we cherished a lot of memories that centered around Gene Autry. As men we added to them. He was the best. It was a perfect week, I wish Lew could have been there.

Chapter Seventeen

Don: Thank you very much and welcome to a Saturday night
in Nashville with the Statler Brothers.
We are the Statler Brothers. I'm Don.

Phil: I'm Phil

Jimmy: I'm Jimmy

Harold: And I'm_____.

— *Don Reid and Harold Reid*

— Don —

And the above mentioned is pretty much how every *Statler Brothers Show* on TNN opened at 9 EST, Saturday nights, on television throughout most of the 90s. But a lot happened before it ever got that far.

Television had been courting us for two decades. We had done three seasons on ABC with *The Johnny Cash Show* in the late 60s and early 70s and had proven that we could do skits, dialogue and comedy and also that we could talk. This may sound meaningless to you, but you'd be surprised at the singers out there who can't even do patter between songs. Can't tell a joke and consequently clam up and just stand there and sing. This works for many of them but it also limits many of them. We had been doing comedy routines that Harold and I wrote from the very beginning when we were still just working churches and banquets back in our hometown. Our stage shows were full of 'shtick' and jokes and impersonations and anything we thought the audience might enjoy as much as we did. We would try anything and this attitude paid off on the Cash TV show as we were handed a lot of special material to do from time to time.

Then Jim Owens, producer, stepped into the picture and took a chance on four people hosting an awards show which had never been done before. Thanks to God and our not knowing that the bumblebee can't fly, we made Jim look like a genius and hosted the *Music City News/TNN Awards Show* for nine years. Through here somewhere, Barbara Mandrell became our opening act and our best friend. While she was traveling with us, Hollywood came calling and she took on an NBC variety show. We wished her well and went out and did the show with her on a number of occasions. Then her producer came calling on us to make the same move. Some people over at ABC, whom we had known from the Cash days, came courting also and we met with and listened to all they had to say, but at the time we just weren't ready to tie ourselves down to a weekly series. And we knew if ever we were ready there were two very important stipulations: (1) we wouldn't move our families and (2) we wanted the freedom to do a show the way we wanted to. In between there were numerous syndicated deals offered us but none of them had the alluring scent at the time.

We did three specials with Jim Owens and Harold and I wrote them; the first one with Pat and Billy Galvin, a man and wife team who wrote for a lot of standup comics, and the other two by ourselves. We performed them the way we felt them and they were very successful. So when Jim came to us with a meeting about a series in April of 1990, we listened because we liked the way he did television. The second meeting was in May and this time he brought the head of the Nashville Network with him. TNN was young and strong and was looking for the very audience we already had. We liked what we heard and went back for more meetings in June and August and on

November 12, 1990, signed a contract with them to do 13 shows starting the fall of 1991.

We got everything we wanted. We got the people we wanted—Bill Walker as our musical director whom we had become close with since the Cash TV show. (Remember John saying "Goodnight, Bill Walker" at the end of every show? Same wonderful man.) We got the director, Steve Womack, who had done all our specials and most of the awards shows we hosted and Jim Stanley as our set director. His men could build anything we could dream up. We got the top production staff headed by old friends Frances Anne Varallo and Pam Repp; Marc Repp was our sound engineer; and we shared executive producer credits with our business partner, Marshall Grant, and Jim. What this all added up to was we had a show and we could do it any way we wanted.

The sound and look of a show is very important and with four males out front every week, we decided we wanted to soften things up a little and hire a female announcer instead of the obvious male voice. We couldn't think of any show that had ever used a woman in this capacity so we began auditioning lady announcers. We came across a jewel named Sherry Paige. A very pretty and talented woman and I suppose we did her an injustice never showing her on camera. But she became such a curiosity with so much mail asking who she was and if we would please put her on so they could see what she looked like, that we played the game and kept her a complete mystery, never letting the camera find her. And here is the irony of it all. She would come in after the shows were taped and mixed and put her voice on. By this time we were off and gone to Virginia or parts unknown and I can honestly say that *I* only laid eyes on her once during the whole run of the series.

The other strange experience early in the game was the hiring of the 'card girls.' We came up with the idea to have a couple of girls, à la old vaudeville, to turn a set of placards on the side of the stage, after each segment, to tell the audience what was coming up next. An old show business ploy to keep the crowd informed and an excuse to utilize a couple of pretty girls. But now being the producers, we had to audition models to find the right two ladies we wanted. Sounds like fun, doesn't it? I won't say it wasn't but it was stressful work. We spent one whole week running girls in a room, asking them questions, watching them walk, listening to them talk, reading resumes and saying, "we'll let you know." I felt like a lecherous old cigar-chewing, back-room Broadway producer and was glad when we found and agreed on two beautiful women, Tamara and Sharon, to become our "Page Girls."

We had always been fans of the variety show genre and learned from the people who had come before us. Jack Benny was brilliant but the supporting cast he kept around him with the likes of Rochester, Dennis Day, and Phil Harris made the show. Garry Moore had Durward Kirby, Marion Lorne, and Carol Burnett. Carol Burnett had Harvey Korman, Lyle Waggoner, and Vicki Lawrence. And I could go on and on but you get the picture. We needed a cast of regulars. People who could sing and carry a three-minute song spot and do special features with us. We needed a 'girl singer' and a 'boy singer.'

Suzy Bogguss was our opening act at the time and our first choice. We pitched her the idea and she loved it but eventually had to drop out of the picture due to record commitments. She's still a good friend and a superb talent and we went to see her in concert not long ago just to watch her sing. We then called Janie Fricke, who had done one of our specials with us. Janie can sing any kind of song better than anybody who has sung it before and she also had a string of her own hits. She took to the idea immediately and that left us with only one slot to fill. One call to an old pal who shared our love of the old movies and who had a voice second only to his dad's and the cast was complete—Rex Allen, Jr. Now we had all we needed except one thing—a script.

Harold and I had written songs and stage routines for years. We had gotten our feet wet with script writing while doing the specials, but we had no idea if we could write a show a week or not. We *said* we could; we just didn't know if we believed ourselves or not. So we sat down after New Year's of '91 at the twenty-foot glass-top table in our conference room, which became our official writing room, at our offices with a handful of pencils, a stop watch and two stacks of blank paper. This was before either one of us was computer-friendly. We wrote every word of every show in long hand on legal pads.

Now Marshall Grant's office was in Hernando, Mississippi, and he booked all the guests for the show. He would call or fax the information to us as he confirmed the acts; we would write the shows, the introductions and the comedy routines, and fax them to our TV staff in Nashville. They would type them up and mail or fax them back to us for approval. So the three major components of putting the show together were stationed in three different states. This was so all of us could sleep in our own beds every night. And it worked. It gave new meaning to long distance and the phone company loved us.

We also chose all the songs for each show and sent them to Bill Walker in Nashville to write the arrangements for our twenty-piece orchestra. And, of course, just when you thought everything was finished, Marshall would call and say a guest had just dropped out and would like to move to another show, and we'd have to tear that one apart and insert someone else and put that guest in another week. We usually had three guests a week: a major singer, a variety act (magician, standup comic, acrobats), and a newcomer or a traditional legend.

It was a wonderful feeling of accomplishment to finish writing a show and send it off but then the next morning that blank sheet of paper was staring at you again waiting for you to start another one. It was the hardest, most stressful, and yet most fulfilling work we've ever done.

★ ★ ★ ★

Our love of nostalgia had played a very prominent part in the songs we had written all our career and we found a way of including that same theme in the TV show. We came up with an idea we called "Yesteryear." Using our cast of regulars, we saluted a year from the past, each week, with music and little facts of history mingled between the songs. Sort of like a mini history lesson with melodies. This took a lot of research and digging for the two of us, but the segment's popularity made it worth it. Janie and Rex fell into the routine as gracefully as if they had been born to it. Phil and Jimmy, who never talked on stage in our concerts, had to take on roles they had never expected. They shared not only the duties of introducing guests with Harold and me, but did an equal share of talk in the "Yesteryear" sketches. They, too, stepped up to the plate and handled it like the pros they are. The talk-throughs were feeling good and come May we had thirteen shows ready to put on videotape.

If the trivia question, "Who was the Statlers' first guest?" ever comes up, it's a complicated answer. Barbara was the guest on the first show, but Conway was the first guest we taped. Sometimes you had to do things out of order to accommodate people's schedules. Those first shows were a love fest for us because then came Roger Miller, Jimmy Dean, Milsap, the Oaks, Charley Pride, Ricky Skaggs, Brenda Lee, Jerry Lee Lewis, and Jerry Reed.

The network ran the show through all the test markets and conference rooms and had it rated and dissected and came back with the report that everyone seemed to like it and that it was ready for the air. We did all the talk show rounds to promote it, went to New York and did satellite hookups and media interviews and come Columbus Day, October 12, 1991, it hit the air. It ranked number one that night on the network and remained as TNN's number one show for the next seven years. We had waited and done television the way we wanted and it paid off. Now all we needed to complete the season were thirteen more shows. It was time for ole Harold and ole Don to get back to work.

★ ★ ★ ★

I mentioned earlier that a stopwatch was one of the essential utensils on our writing table. Maybe I should explain. When writing a song, it can run anywhere from three to six minutes and still be acceptable. In writing a book, it's all measured by pages in round numbers. You may write a joke that's two minutes long or maybe it's a one-liner. There is no set rule on how long any creative writing should be… except in television. In the world of the magic box everything has to come out to the second! No hedging, no cheating. You've got to get the commercials in and it's all timed down to the tick. In a sixty minute television show, sixteen minutes are for the advertisers. That leaves you forty-four minutes of entertainment. And it's relevant. In a thirty minute show you only have twenty-two minutes of entertainment. This can't vary. If you run over you chop songs or chop introductions or some piece of business that you worked all night on. This is where the pressure comes in. If it's short, stretch it. If it's long, cut it. Most times we handled this at the writing level, but sometimes it had to be handled on the air. If a guest ran long with their song or a comic had a lapse in memory and left a joke out of his routine, we had to make it up at the end of the show with a quick "goodnight" or something funny to fill in the time. The good thing about the latter is that some of the best stuff is created on the spot out of necessity. And the bad thing is that some of the best stuff is lost on the cutting room floor out of that same necessity.

★ ★ ★ ★

The first thing that had to be addressed was our touring schedule. We usually worked approximately one hundred concerts a year. Not as many as a lot of folks in our industry, but the demand was always there and we found turning a city down just made them more determined to have you next year.

We could easily have worked *three* hundred days a year but those who do find themselves married to a bus and living in a hotel room. We enjoyed our lives and always tried to plan our fun time as well as our work. We discovered years before that if you let the work dictate your schedule you'd never get to Disney World with the kids. So to keep ourselves from overloading our circuits, we cut our concerts back to approximately forty per year. This allowed Harold and me time to write the shows, and then perform them and then start producing the next batch. One season ran into another and to be completely honest, we would have served ourselves well if we had just stopped touring altogether during the run of the television show. But we had a band and drivers and remembering back to the Roy Acuff story and how he was working so the band could, we found ourselves in the same situation. To appease the cut back in touring days, we had our five-piece band on one half of all of our shows even though we were also paying an orchestra to be there every week. We always tried to be considerate and more than fair on every front.

★ ★ ★ ★

When we started the show, we had three years in mind. We figured it would be fun and interesting for a while and then we'd drop it and put more attention back on our records and concerts. But after three seasons, it was so popular and so much fun, not to mention so much work, that we decided to stay with it another year or two. Every meeting we had with the network would end with them asking if we had any other ideas for other shows we would like to produce. In giving this some thought, we had noticed the fan mail and how much the public liked the "Yesteryear" segment. They really got into it and loved trying to guess what year we would reveal at the end. So we knocked around the idea of spinning off that eight minute piece of the show and making it a series of its own. We would produce it and the next step would be finding the right stars to carry it. Our obvious choices were the people who had proven themselves to be so good at it week after week, Rex and Janie. Rex went for it immediately but Janie decided not to take that leap, so we hired a beautiful and talented, up-and-coming girl at the time, Lisa Stewart. The network liked them, we liked them, and now we were officially TV producers with multi-shows on the air. Well, not quite on the air. We still needed a script for *Yesteryear* so Harold and I, instead of hiring two writers, again said we would do it not knowing exactly where the time would be found to fulfill that promise. But the Lord always looks after fools and overextended writers and He came through for us again.

1994 was a blur for us all. We had sort of thrown all our work policies to the wind and were knee-deep in two TV productions. We wrote and finished taping one half of the Statler Brothers shows in Nashville by the end of February. We came home and started the next day writing the entire *Yesteryear* series, twenty-six shows, and had it ready to go in front of the cameras by July, which had always been our vacation month. As soon as the last note was sung, we left Nashville and headed home again to begin writing the second half of the Statler Brothers shows which were due to begin taping in Nashville in November. And in between the cracks we still managed to do forty-one concerts that year.

It got to the point where the two of us had to carry our writing office with us. We bought a big steamer trunk and packed all of our writing materials and research books in it and carried that ridiculous thing into hotels every morning so we could write all day, do the show that night and load up and start all over the next dawn. All the books were history and fact books used to create new segments to take the place of the "Yesteryear" spot we had now designated to the new series. We came up with "Music Mail Time," answering song requests from the public and giving a little background on each song before we sang it; "State Salutes" where we honored different states with songs written about the state or by songwriters from the state and always closing with the singing of the state song; "Artist Salutes" where we honored the career of country legends and sang their big hits just before bringing them out in person to sing their biggest; and "Hollywood" featuring music from old movies.

We did a new Christmas show every other season. We did a World War II special to honor the 50-year anniversary of D-Day. We did an all-magic show where our only guests were magicians and every song sung on the show had the word magic in the title. We did a 50s show and dressed accordingly, sang all 50s songs and made sure we had authentic 50s guests: Pat Boone and Teresa Brewer. Is that authentic enough?

When Janie left and Rex went to *Yesteryear*, we replaced them with Crystal Gayle and Ronna Reeves. Crystal, already a major star and Ronna, the newcomer, gave the look a perfect balance with four guys and two girls. We put a lot of stock in our regulars and the final season we were rotating some heavyweight performers in those spots. For three or four weeks we'd have Connie Smith and Pat Boone and the next few weeks we'd have Linda Davis and Glen Campbell. It was a highly creative and happy time. Everybody was loving what we were doing and we felt as comfortable in television as we ever felt on stage.

A national Harris Poll was taken in 1996 to determine America's favorite singers and these were the top ten:

1. Frank Sinatra
2. The Statler Brothers
3. Reba McEntire
4. Garth Brooks
5. Whitney Houston
6. Vince Gill
7. Barbra Streisand
8. The Beatles
9. Alan Jackson
10. Michael Jackson

Oh, what the heck. We'll take second place to "ole blue eyes" any day.

★ ★ ★ ★

You've probably always heard that ratings were the things that kept TV shows on the air. Don't believe it. There is something else more important and it's called demographics. No matter how high your ratings are, if the right people aren't watching, you're vulnerable to the business graphs of the advertising department. If you don't believe me just ask Angela Lansbury. *Murder She Wrote* finished with high ratings for twelve seasons but the people watching were just too old. The same fate befell Jane Seymour with *Dr. Quinn, Medicine Woman*. The television graveyard is full of these same stories. Every network is looking for that 18 − 30 year old audience. If you have millions in the 35 − 50 year old crowd, which we did, you're eventually going to run into problems. They don't care how many households are out there waiting on you on Saturday night; they only care what their age is and what they'll spend their money on.

After our seventh season of being number one (our *Yesteryear* show was number two its entire run), we went in for a breakfast meeting with TNN's managing vice-president, Brian Hughes, to negotiate an eighth season. Before we even ordered the eggs, he said, "I have something I have to tell you and after I do, you may not want to eat breakfast with me." He told us we were being cancelled. He even offered to put out a news release saying we had quit if that would suit our situation better. We refused his offer and told him we weren't about to lie to our public. I think that magnanimous gesture was so they wouldn't have to take the heat and get all the negative mail they knew was in the offing.

We all stood up, shook hands and hugged, and then sat back down and we bought him breakfast.

★ ★ ★ ★

We have some wonderful memories of that TV show: the seven years of friendships we made, the guest stars that came and gave their best, the new fans we met, and the creative stretching we called on one another to constantly live up to. We laughed at our mistakes and even left some of them in so the audience could laugh at them, too. We tackled music we never would have had reason to approach if not for the shear volume of songs we had to learn in a year's span. We had so many of our heroes from the pop and country and gospel fields and made sure that the old-timers, the legends in those fields, were showcased better on camera and treated better backstage than they had been in years. We visited with every guest in their dressing room and welcomed them to the show and ate dinner with them and had our pictures taken with them before they left the building, leaving them with an understanding of just what their presence meant to us.

And we walked away from those wonderful years better than we arrived, richer in friends and relationships and fuller of spirit in knowing that we had done something that made America smile and enjoy themselves, if only for a few minutes, every Saturday night.

Chapter Eighteen

All the helloes and the goodbyes, they're just today
All the thank yous and I love yous, just something we say
All the night walks and the bed talks that kept our dreams alive
And what will you remember when you are sixty-five
— Don Reid
"When You're Sixty-Five"

— Harold —

There was nothing in our career that was more satisfying than our television years. I guess I had finally learned how to work hard and enjoy it at the same time. But it was the end of an era and I was well aware of it. My mind is very symmetrical and divides everything into categories. Performing, recording, writing, producing, and publishing are all nice accomplishments and I felt we had done them all successfully. Also, I have a real thing about never over-staying your welcome. That goes for hit records, television shows or visiting someone in the hospital. You should know how to enter and when to leave. I guess that kind of thinking was in play for me when the TV show was over. Also, I knew we just weren't eighteen years old anymore.

It had happened during one of our TV tapings in Nashville. Phil had remarked the cue cards were too far away. Later, he said they were blurred and finally that he couldn't read them at all. He came home the next week and after extensive testing was diagnosed with sugar diabetes. He started his regimen of insulin injections and to this day has trouble with totally controlling the sugar levels. It's certainly not his fault because there's no one more committed to exercise and blood checks. It's been rough, but Phil, being who he is, never complains. That's Phil. He never sits around thinking about himself. He has suffered blackout effects from his condition but still called to check on me because I had a head cold.

Phil is easy to take for granted. He is agreeable, cooperative and does his job better than anybody else. He handles it all with the same attitude. He's concerned but not a worrier. He's talented without being proud. He knows the answer before he hears the question, but unlike me, he waits till you ask his opinion. I said it before, he's a gentleman and he's my buddy and I love him. So I hated to see him fighting an unyielding disease. Put all this together and you could put the blame on me to first mention retirement. I felt we had accomplished more than our dreams and certainly more than we deserved. We had prayed for a little. God had given us a lot.

We could all still walk, talk, sing and had shared our lives with our wonderful supporters all those years. Now it was time to go home and thank my girl, Brenda, who had done most of the work while I got all the applause. Maybe hug the kids, Kim, Karmen, Kodi, Kasey, and Wil, who had given up some of their life so Dad could shine. And maybe tell some old-man stories to my grandkids, Rob, Sid, Beth, John Reid, Alex, Lexi, Wilson, and Jackson. After all, I'd better tell them while I still remember.

But most of all I didn't want me nor any of my Brothers to be an eighty year-old performer who couldn't carry a tune. I've seen it happen. Some people stay too long and forever more you remember them for what they became rather than what they became famous for. My Brothers didn't totally agree.

— Don —

It was the summer of 1998, the same summer the TV show had been cancelled. Harold and I were alone in the lounge of the bus late one night and he confided to me he just wasn't ready to resume a full touring schedule again. He said he was thinking about hanging it up and I told him from the beginning I felt he should follow his heart but I wasn't sure I was at that point yet. Months went by before the subject came up again and this time Phil was with us. Phil said very little except that he felt the same as me. I'm six years younger than Harold and Phil so that might explain some of my feelings. Jimmy is younger than all of us, so we knew he had no interest in this kind of thinking. He had only been doing this for half the time we had and everything he was doing he was doing for the first time, so it was still fresh and new and exciting for him.

The subject continued to come up with the three of us and for the next few years we struggled with how we could cut back on dates to please everyone and yet work enough to please everyone else and there was just no solution. After many meetings with Marshall and Butch Hupp, our trusted business advisor, we decided to make the announcement to our employees and the public a year in advance. (We had done this same thing when we stepped away from our Fourth of July celebration. We gave the public a five-year notice so everyone would have a chance to come who wanted to come.) This would give our staff and our band ample notice to find new work and afford the loyal fans a whole year's opportunity to catch our last annual tour. And those fans were still very loyal. The crowds never faded. We were playing to SRO theaters and auditoriums and arenas right up to the end. This is why the industry was puzzled by our move. They couldn't understand how we could, or why we would, walk away from a still booming career that generated what it did each year. I have been in country music all my life, since I was eighteen years old, and I have known only a handful of artists who have retired at their peak and meant it: Sonny James, Barbara Mandrell, and The Statlers. (Others have promised to quit but they just won't completely go away.)

So after a four-year discussion of if and how and when, we bought into Harold's wisdom to exit from the top while we were still young and healthy enough to enjoy the fruits of retirement. We told our people, our families and our co-workers, and every night of that final year, we told our fans. We told them we wouldn't be back. That this was the last time we'd ever be in their town and the last time we would ever see their faces or hear their applause. We pulled out of each city that year with a stealth and quietness that encompassed the whole atmosphere. We weren't sad; we were just very aware. We set the final date for Salem, Virginia, and broke all house records there for attendance. The closer it got, the easier it got. I think we were as ready and pumped for the winding down as we were for the winding up that long-ago night in Canton, Ohio, when we first joined the Johnny Cash Show.

Chapter One

. . . That was my final thought just before I heard "Ladies and Gentlemen, the Statler Brothers" for the last time. That was what was rushing through my mind as I followed the other three on the stage and into the lights that night... "Where are those kids and how did they get to be these men and why is everybody standing and clapping?"

And after reading these pages, you know now where those kids went and how they got to be those men. And after writing these pages, we realize that it was all a dream. A dream that never stopped even when we woke up. A dream that constantly surprised us year after year after year. A dream we never quite allowed ourselves to totally believe.

And we still don't quite understand why all those people were standing and clapping. But we're grateful to God they did.

Thanks,

Harold & Don

DISCOGRAPHY

Albums

Columbia

Flowers On The Wall 1966
Flowers On The Wall★
My Darling Hildegard★
King Of The Road
Memphis
I'm Not Quite Through Crying
My Reward
This Ole House
The Ballad Of Billy Christian
The Doodlin' Song
Quite A Long, Long Time
The Whiffenpoof Song
I Still Miss Someone

The Statler Brothers Sing The Big Hits 1967
Ruthless★
You Can't Have Your Kate And Edith, Too★
Release Me
Walking In The Sunshine
Funny, Familiar, Forgotten Feelings
Ruby, Don't Take Your Love To Town
Green, Green Grass Of Home
There Goes My Everything
Almost Persuaded
I Can't Help It If I'm Still In Love With You
Shenandoah

How Great Thou Art 1969
How Great Thou Art
O Happy Day★
King Of Love
Are You Washed In The Blood
The Things God Gave Me
Just In Time
Led Out Of Bondage
The Fourth Man
Pass Me Not
Less Of Me

During this five-year period at Columbia, other singles were released that were not included on these three original albums but would subsequently show up on future compilation albums: "The Right One," " That'll Be The Day," "Sissy," "Jump For Joy," "I'm The Boy," "Hammers And Nails," "Green Grass," "Do You Love Me Tonight?" "Is That What You'd Have Me Do?" "Makin' Rounds," "Half A Man," "Staunton, VA."

Mercury

Bed Of Rose's 1970
Bed Of Rose's★
New York City★
All I Have To Offer You Is Me
Neighborhood Girl
Fifteen Years Ago
The Junkie's Prayer
We
This Part Of The World
Tomorrow Never Comes
Me And Bobby McGee
The Last Goodbye

Pictures Of Moments To Remember 1971

You Can't Go Home★
Second Thoughts
Tender Years
Faded Love
Makin' Memories
Things
Pictures★
When You And I Were Young, Maggie
Just Someone I Used To Know
I Wonder How The Old Folks Are At Home
Moments To Remember

Innerview 1972

Do You Remember These?★
I'd Rather Be Sorry
Every Day Will Be Sunday
Bye And Bye
She Thinks I Still Care
Got Leavin' On Her Mind
I'll Take Care Of You
Take Me Home, Country Roads
Daddy
Never Ending Song Of Love
A Different Song
Since Then

Country Music Then And Now 1972

When My Blue Moon Turns To Gold
No One Will Ever Know
Saturday Morning Radio Show
Class Of '57★
A Stranger In My Place
Jesus, Take Another Look At Me
1953-Dear John-Honky Tonk Blues
Under It All
Every Time I Trust A Gal

Country Symphonies In E Major 1973

Monday Morning Secretary★
Burning Bridges
I Wanna Carry Your Sweet Memories
I Believe In Music
A Special Song For Wanda
I'll Be Your Baby Tonight
Woman Without A Home★
Delta Dawn
Wedding Bells
Too Many Rivers
They Can't Take You Out Of Me

Carry Me Back 1973

Carry Me Back★
The Woman I Still Love
What Do I Care
If We Never Had
Take Good Care Of Her
The Streets Of San Francisco
Whatever Happened To Randolph Scott★
I Wish I Could Be
We Owe It All To Yesterday
When I Stop Dreaming
The Strand

Thank You, World 1974

Thank You, World★
City Lights
Sweet Charlotte Ann
Left-Handed Woman
The Blackwood Brothers By The Statler Brothers
Cowboy Buckaroo
She's Too Good
The Baptism Of Jesse Taylor
Streets Of Baltimore
Margie's At The Lincoln Park Inn
The Boy Inside Of Me

Sons Of The Motherland   1974
So Mary Could Make It Home
A Letter From Shirley Miller
All-American Girl★
Eight More Miles To Louisville
One More Summer In Virginia
You've Been Like A Mother To Me
A Few Old Memories
I'll Be Here
Susan When She Tried★
Together
You Can't Judge A Book By Its Cover

Alive At The Johnny Mack Brown High School
1974

A comedy album written and performed by the Statlers
in the guise of Lester Moran and the Cadillac Cowboys

The Best Of The Statler Brothers   1975
(Gold/Triple Platinum)
I'll Go To My Grave Loving You★
Bed Of Rose's
Class Of '57
Flowers On The Wall
Thank You, World
Whatever Happened To
  Randolph Scott
Do You Remember These?
Carry Me Back
Pictures
New York City
Susan When She Tried

The Holy Bible – Old Testament   1975
(Gold)
In The Beginning
Eve
Noah Found Grace In The Eyes
  Of The Lord
Have A Little Faith
The Dreamer
Led Out Of Bondage
The Ten Commandments
Samson
Song Of David
Song Of Solomon
The Fourth Man
The King Is Coming

The Holy Bible – New Testament   1975
(Gold)
Who Do You Think
The Kingdom Of Heaven Is At Hand
Beat The Devil
The Brave Apostles Twelve
The Teacher
The Lord's Prayer
There's A Man In Here
How Great Thou Art★
Lord, Is It I?
The King Of Love
The King Is Coming

Harold, Lew, Phil, And Don 1976
Your Picture In The Paper★
All The Times
Something I Haven't Done Yet
The Times We Had
I've Been Everywhere
Amanda
A Friend's Radio
Maggie
Virginia
Would You Recognize Jesus
The Statler Brothers Quiz

The Country America Loves 1977
Hat And Boots
Thank God I've Got You★
The Movies★
Let It Show
You Could Be Coming To Me
Blue Eyes Crying In The Rain
You Comb Her Hair
I Was There★
A Couple More Years
All I Can Do
Somebody New Will Be Coming Along

Short Stories 1977
Silver Medals And Sweet Memories★
The Regular Saturday Night Setback Card Game
That Summer
He Went To The Cross Loving You
Quite A Long, Long Time
Carried Away
The Star
Grandma
Different Things To Different People
Give My Love To Rose
Some I Wrote★

Entertainers On And Off The Record 1978
(Gold)
Do You Know You Are My Sunshine★
Who Am I to Say★
The Official Historian On Shirley Jean Berrell★
The Best I Can Do
I Dreamed About You
I Forgot More Than You'll Ever Know About Her
You're The First
Yours Love
Before The Magic Turns To Memory
When You're 65
Tomorrow Is Your Friend

Christmas Card 1978
(Gold/Platinum)
I Believe In Santa's Cause★
I'll Be Home For Christmas
Jingle Bells
White Christmas
I Never Spend A Christmas That I Don't Think Of You★
Christmas To Me
Who Do You Think
Away In A Manger
Something You Can't Buy
The Carol Those Kids Used To Sing
A Christmas Medley

The Originals 1979
(Gold)

How To Be A Country Star★
When The Yankees Came Home
A Little Farther Down The Road
Here We Are Again★
Mr. Autry
The Star-Spangled Banner
Almost In Love
Nothing As Original As You★
A Little Talk With Jesus
Counting My Memories
Where He's Always Wanted To Be

The Best Of The Statler Brothers Rides Again
1979 (Gold)

(I'll Even Love You) Better Than
  I Did Then★
Do You Know You Are My Sunshine
Here We Are Again
The Movies
Your Picture In The Paper
Some I Wrote
How Great Thou Art
How To Be A Country Star
Silver Medals And Sweet Memories
Who Am I To Say
The Official Historian On Shirley Jean Berrell

Tenth Anniversary 1980
(Gold)

Don't Forget Yourself★
The Kid's Last Fight
How Are Things In Clay, Kentucky
One Less Day To Go
Nobody Wants To Be Country
We Got Paid By Cash
Old Cheerleaders Cry
Till The End
Nobody's Darlin' But Mine
Charlotte's Web★

Years Ago 1981

Years Ago★
Don't Wait On Me★
Today I Went Back
In The Garden★
Chet Atkins' Hands
You'll Be Back Every Night In My Dreams★
Love Was All We Had
We Ain't Even Started Yet
Dad
Memories Are Made Of This

The Legend Goes On 1982

Child Of The Fifties★
What You Are To Me
How Do You Like Your Dream So Far
I Don't Know Why
That's When It Comes Home To You
I'll Love You All Over Again
Life's Railway To Heaven
I Don't Dance No More
Whatever★
I Had Too Much To Dream

Today 1983
(Gold)
O Baby Mine★
Some Memories Last Forever
Promise
I'm Dying A Little Each Day
There is You
Guilty★
Elizabeth★
Right On The Money
I Never Want To Kiss You Goodbye
In the Sweet By And By

Atlanta Blue 1984
(Gold)
Atlanta Blue★
If It Makes Any Difference
Let's Just Take One Night At A Time
Anger In Her Face
Hollywood
One Takes The Blame★
Give It Your Best
No Love Lost
One Size Fits All
My Only Love★

Pardners In Rhyme 1985
(Gold)
Hello Mary Lou★
Sweeter And Sweeter★
Memory Lane
Remembering You
Too Much On My Heart★
I'm Sorry You Had To Be The One
Her Heart Or Mine
You Don't Wear Blue So Well
Autumn Leaves
Amazing Grace

Christmas Present 1985
Christmas Eve (Kodia's Theme)★
Christmas Country Style
Brahms' Bethlehem Lullaby
Somewhere In The Night
An Old-Fashioned Christmas
No Reservation At The Inn
Mary's Sweet Smile
Whose Birthday Is Christmas
Old Toy Trains
For Momma

Four For The Show 1986
Count On Me★
You Oughta Be Here With Me
We Got The Memories
I Don't Dream Anymore
Forever★
Only You★
For Cryin' Out Loud
Will You Be There
I Believe I'll Live For Him
More Like My Daddy Than Me

Radio Gospel Favorites 1986
(Gold)
There Is Power In The Blood
We Won't Be Home Until Then
One Size Fits All
In The Sweet By And By
I Believe I'll Live For Him
A Different Song
Blessed Be
A Beautiful Life
Amazing Grace
Over The Sunset Mountain

Maple Street Memories   1987
Our Street / Tell Me Why
Maple Street Memories★
Déjà Vu
Am I Crazy★
The Best I Know How★
I'll Be the One★
Beyond Romance
I Lost my Heart to You
Jesus Showed Me So

The Statler Brothers' Greatest Hits Vol III   1988
Let's Get Started If We're Gonna Break My Heart★
Elizabeth
Count On Me
The Best I Know How
Moon Pretty Moon★
More Than A Name On A Wall★
Guilty
My Only Love
I'll Be The One
Atlanta Blue

Live and Sold Out 1989
Walking Heartache In Disguise★
The Official Historian
  On Shirley Jean Berrell
Bed Of Rose's
Foggy Mountain Breakdown
A Hurt I Can't Handle★
I'll Fly Away
Tomorrow Never Comes
Don't Wait On Me
This Ole House
When The Roll Is Called Up Yonder
I'll Go To My Grave Loving You

Music, Memories And You 1990
Small, Small World★
Nobody Else★
Jealous Eyes
Holding On
Think Of Me
You Gave Yourself Away
I Never Once Got Tired Of You
What's On My Mind
He Is There
My Music, My Memories And You

All-American Country 1991
Remember Me★
Dynamite
Everything You See In Your Dreams
Who Do You Think You Are
There's Still Time★
Put It On The Card
If I'd Paid More Attention To You
Jesus Is The Answer Every Time
Fallin' In Love
You've Been Like A Mother To Me★

Words And Music 1992
Too Make A Long Story Short
It Only Hurts For A Little While
A Lifetime Of Loving You In Vain★
The Rest Of My Life
Some I Wrote
Nobody Loves Here Anymore
Same Way Everytime★
Is It Your Place Or Mine
He's Always There For You
Thank You For Breaking My Heart

Gospel Favorites (TV Double Album) 1992
(Gold)
When the Roll Is Called Up Yonder
Rock Of Ages
Noah Found Grace In The Eyes Of The Lord
The Old Rugged Cross
Blessed Be
One Size Fits All
In The Sweet By And By
Turn Your Radio On
Amazing Grace
Love Lifted Me
There Is Power In The Blood
This Ole House

- - - - -

Precious Memories
How Great Thou Art
Jesus Is The Answer Every Time
Over The Sunset Mountain
I Believe I'll Live For Him
In The Garden
A Different Song
Just A Little Talk With Jesus
A Beautiful Life
I'll Fly Away

Home 1993
The All-Girl-All-Gospel Quartet
Chattanooga Shoe Shine Boy★
He'll Always Have You Again
Feelin' Mighty Fine
My Past Is Looking Brighter
That Haunted Ole House
Chet, You're The Reason
I've Never Lived This Long Before
What We Love To Do★

A 30th Anniversary Celebration 1994

The Essential Statler Brothers 3-Disc Box Set with pictures, booklet and 62 songs spanning thirty years of music.

The Statler Brothers Sing the Classics (TV Double Album) 1995

Memories Are Made Of This
The Great Pretender
Gone
Naughty Lady Of Shady Lane
She Thinks I Still Care
I'll Go To My Grave Loving You
Moments To Remember
Chattanooga Shoe Shine Boy
Making Believe
Tom Dooley
Love Letters In The Sand
Hello Mary Lou

- - - - -

Unchained Melody
The Battle Of New Orleans
I Can't Stop Loving You
Bye, Bye Love
Only You
Have I Told You Lately That I Love You
O Baby Mine
It Only Hurts For A Little While
He's Got The Whole World In His Hands
Bed Of Rose's
Love Me Tender
Goodnight, Sweetheart

Pulp Fiction (Sound Track Album) 1995
(Platinum)
Flowers On The Wall

Music Box

Showtime 2001
She Never Altogether Leaves
Too Late For The Roses
You Just Haven't Done It Yet
In Love With You
Too Long Ago
All I'll Need From You
Darlin' I Do
I've Had A Good Time
It Should Have Been Me ★
Look At Me
The Other Side Of The Cross
I've Got Jesus On My Side

Amen 2003
A Place On Calvary
Hide Thou Me
It Might Be Jesus
He's Getting Me Ready
God Saw My Need
Keep Your Eyes On Jesus
Jesus Living Next To Me
If It Only Took A Baby
The Far Side Banks Of Jordan
When I Take My Vacation In Heaven
I Should Have Known You, Lord
A Living Part Of You

Yell

Farewell Concert (Live Album) 2003

Do You Remember These?
Do You Know You Are My Sunshine
Susan When She Tried
Too Much On My Heart
Class Of '57
Bed Of Rose's
O Baby Mine
Moments To Remember
Memories Are Made Of This
The Great Pretender
Whatever Happened To Randolph Scott
More Than A Name On A Wall
Flowers On The Wall
Elizabeth
I'll Go To My Grave Loving You
Bus Fumes
A Place On Calvary
How Great Thou Art
This Ole House
Thank You, World
Amazing Grace
(Includes comedy routines and final goodbyes)

These were the original albums The Statlers recorded and released during their career. Many other albums were subsequently released and are still being released by these labels plus Time-Life, Heartland, etc., but they are compilation albums, meaning projects created by using already recorded and previously released material.
★ Denotes singles from the listed album.

MAJOR AWARDS

The Statlers received over 550 awards in their nearly 40-year career and were often referred to as the most awarded act in the history of country music. Below are listed a few of the major awards they received.

Grammy®	Best New Country Group	1965
Grammy®	Best Contemporary Performance by a Group	1965
Grammy®	Best Country Performance by a Group	1972

CMA (Country Music Association)	Group of the Year	1972, 1973, 1974, 1975, 1976, 1977 1979, 1980, 1984

ACM (Academy of Country Music)	Group of the Year	1972, 1978

People's Choice	Favorite Group	1983, 1987

AMA (American Music Awards)	Group of the Year	1979, 1980, 1981

MCN/TNN	Group of the Year	1971, 1972, 1973, 1974, 1975, 1976
(Music City News/The Nashville Network)		1977, 1978, 1979, 1980, 1981,1982
		1984, 1985, 1986, 1987, 1988, 1989
		1990, 1991, 1992, 1993, 1994, 1996
		1997
Entertainer of the Year		1983, 1986, 1987
Album of the Year		1979, 1980, 1981, 1985, 1986
Single of the Year		1984, 1986, 1987, 1990
TV Special of the Year		1982, 1984, 1986
Comedy Act of the Year		1980, 1982, 1983, 1984, 1985
Video of the Year		1985, 1986, 1988

Induction into The Gospel Music Association Hall of Fame	2007

ABOUT THE AUTHORS

Harold Reid and **Don Reid** are members of The Statler Brothers, the most award-winning act in the history of country music and one of the premier singing groups in America for nearly 40 years. Songwriters, television writers and performers, these Grammy® Award winning brothers are now retired from touring, and are living the good life exemplified by so much of their music.

Harold lives with his wife, Brenda, in Staunton, Virginia. This is his first published book.

Don, who has authored three previous books, lives with his wife, Debbie, in Staunton, Virginia.

Permissions

Song lyrics reprinted by the permission of the copyright owner:

"Do You Remember These?"
(Larry Lee, Don Reid, Harold Reid)
House of Cash Inc. BMI

"Class of '57"
(Harold Reid, Don Reid)
House of Cash Inc. BMI

"So Mary Could Make It Home"
(Don Reid)
Songs of Universal, Inc. BMI

"I'll Go To My Grave Loving You"
(Don Reid)
Songs of Universal, Inc. BMI

"He Went To The Cross Loving You"
(Don Reid, Harold Reid)
Songs of Universal, Inc. BMI

"You've Been Like A Mother To Me"
(Don Reid)
Songs of Universal, Inc. BMI

"The Statler Brothers Quiz"
(Harold Reid, Don Reid)
Songs of Universal, Inc. BMI

"Flowers On The Wall"
(Lewis DeWitt)
Unichappell Music Inc./Wallflower Music BMI

"How To Be A Country Star"
(Don Reid, Harold Reid)
Songs of Universal, Inc. BMI

"Do You Know You Are My Sunshine"
(Harold Reid, Don Reid)
Songs of Universal, Inc. BMI

"Don't Wait On Me"
(Don Reid, Harold Reid)
Songs of Universal, Inc. BMI

Whatever Happened To Randolph Scott"
(Harold Reid, Don Reid)
Songs of Universal, Inc. BMI

"When The Yankees Came Home"
(Don Reid)
Songs of Universal, Inc. BMI

"Bed Of Rose's"
(Harold Reid)
House of Cash Inc./Songs of Universal, Inc. BMI

"The Blackwood Brothers
By The Statler Brothers"
(Don Reid)
Songs of Universal, Inc. BMI

"All American Girl"
(Don Reid, Harold Reid)
Songs of Universal, Inc. BMI

"Silver Medals And Sweet Memories"
(Don Reid)
Songs of Universal, Inc. BMI

"Elizabeth"
(Jimmy Fortune)
Songs of Universal, Inc. BMI

"Guilty"
(Harold Reid, Don Reid)
Songs of Universal, Inc. BMI

Permissions

"The Last Goodbye"
(Harold Reid, Phil Balsley, Lew DeWitt,
Don Reid)
House of Cash Inc./Wallflower Music BMI

"Mary's Sweet Smile"
(Harold Reid, Phil Balsley, Jimmy Fortune,
Don Reid)
Songs of Universal, Inc. BMI

"Mr. Autry"
(Don Reid, Harold Reid)
Songs of Universal, Inc. BMI

"Susan When She Tried"
(Don Reid)
Songs of Universal, Inc. BMI

"These Things Shall Pass"
(Stuart Hamblen)
Songs of Universal, Inc. BMI

"The Times We Had"
(Don Reid)
Songs of Universal, Inc. BMI

"We Got Paid By Cash"
(Harold Reid, Don Reid)
Songs of Universal, Inc. BMI

"Virginia"
(Don Reid, Harold Reid)
Songs of Universal, Inc. BMI

"The Star"
(Don Reid)
Songs of Universal, Inc. BMI

"We"
(Don Reid)
House of Cash Inc. BMI

"Where He Always Wanted To Be"
(Harold Reid, Don Reid)
Songs of Universal, Inc. BMI

"You Can't Go Home"
(Don Reid)
House of Cash Inc. BMI

"How Do You Like Your Dream So Far"
(Don Reid, Harold Reid)
Songs of Universal, Inc. BMI

"We Owe It All To Yesterday"
(Harold Reid, Don Reid)
Songs of Universal, Inc. BMI

"Carry Me Back"
(Don Reid, Harold Reid)
Songs of Universal, Inc. BMI

"Some I Wrote"
(Harold Reid, Don Reid)
Songs of Universal, Inc. BMI

"I've Never Lived This Long Before"
(Don Reid, Harold Reid)
Beverley Manor Music Inc. BMI

"When You're Sixty-Five"
(Don Reid)
Slapich Music BMI

Index

Index

Index

Index

Index

Index